THE GOSPEL COMES TO LIFE

LECTIO DIVINA WITH THE
SUNDAY GOSPEL READINGS

Be Vigilant!

THE GOSPEL COMES TO LIFE

LECTIO DIVINA WITH THE SUNDAY GOSPEL READINGS

Be Vigilant!

YEAR C

(2025, 2028, 2031)

Kevin Saunders

AMERICAN BIBLE SOCIETY

Philadelphia

BE VIGILANT! LECTIO DIVINA FOR YEAR C (The Gospel Comes to Life)

Written by Kevin Saunders
Edited by Peter Edman

For more Bible resources, visit Bibles.com

In this series:
THE GOSPEL COMES TO LIFE
LECTIO DIVINA WITH THE SUNDAY GOSPEL READINGS

STAY AWAKE! (Matthew, Year A, 2023, 2026, 2029)
Paperback Print on Demand   ISBN 978-1-58516-426-4 (Item 125537)
PDF Digital Download   ISBN 978-1-58516-427-1 (Item 125538)

BE ALERT! (Mark, Year B, 2024, 2027, 2030)
Paperback Print on Demand   ISBN 978-1-58516-428-8 (Item 125539)
PDF Digital Download   ISBN 978-1-58516-429-5 (Item 125540)

BE VIGILANT! (Luke, Year C, 2025, 2028, 2031)
Paperback Print on Demand   ISBN 978-1-58516-430-1 (Item 125541)
PDF Digital Download   ISBN 978-1-58516-431-8 (Item 125542)

AMERICAN BIBLE SOCIETY
101 North Independence Mall East, FL8
Philadelphia, PA 19106

americanbible.org

Paperback POD: ISBN 978-1-58516-430-1 (Item 125541)
PDF Digital Download: ISBN 978-1-58516-431-8 (Item 125542)

CONTENTS

PREFACE

WELCOME to this encounter with the Scriptures. I am a Catholic Bible teacher who offers a course through the entire Bible, read aloud and commented upon by me, every chapter of every book over the course of a seven-year journey through the sacred text.

My love for and fascination with the Bible was enhanced during my course of study in Israel. I was blessed to serve the Hebrew University of Jerusalem (Mt. Scopus Campus) as the chaplain for the Christian students there. My position allowed me the opportunity to attend and participate in graduate-level courses on the Bible led by the preeminent scholars of the day. In these seminars I was introduced to the cultural world of the Middle East and how this worldview can reveal the deeper meaning of otherwise challenging texts.

How can the dead bury the dead? How can Jesus expect his disciples to hate their parents if they are going to love him? And how can a camel ever pass through the eye of a needle? These (and other) teachings of Jesus were meaningless to me until Jewish scholars at the university opened the door to the culture of Jesus and how that culture informs his teaching. My understanding of the Bible took off like a rocket from there.

In 2017, American Bible Society asked me to create a series of Lectio Divina reflections based on the Gospel readings for each Sunday in the liturgical calendar. I was thrilled with the invitation, not knowing where the opportunity might lead. Well, the result is *The Gospel Comes to Life,* a three-volume collection of my Lectio offerings for the three cycles of the Catholic Christian sequence of Sunday Gospel readings.

Four principles guide my reflections.

1. *The Bible is rooted in geography.* Understanding the geographic limits and features of the Middle East often guides insights into the Bible.

2. *The Bible emerges from history.* Real people, in real places, do real things that include their response to their culture and environment as well as to God.

3. *The Bible is informed by Middle Eastern culture and custom.* Honor and shame are two key cultural values that direct the narrative.

4. *The Bible is the Word of God,* whole and entire, and is God's final word to humanity.

The reader will note evidence of each of these four principles in my writing. I hope these Lectio reflections will inspire you to dive deeper into the Bible—and into the culture of the Middle East, for its customs reveal much of who Jesus was, is, and will forever be.

It has been a blessing and an honor to complete the reflections that you have in front of you. My prayer for you—as you read, meditate, pray, and apply the Gospel lessons to your life—is that you will grow in faith as much as I have done in creating each Lectio.

I am indebted to American Bible Society for offering me the opportunity to write these Lectios and to the staff who edited my musings week by week over three years. A writer is only as good as his editor and mine have been the best! It has been wonderful to work with ABS and I look forward to more fruitful engagements in the future. Until then, blessings!

KEVIN SAUNDERS
Phoenix, Arizona
March 2023

INTRODUCTION

Lectio Divina means "divine reading" in Latin. It is an approach to Bible reading that invites you to slow down and tune out the noise (from within and without) by inspiring and equipping you to sit in silence and listen for God's voice in Scripture. This way of reading and praying through Scripture has been practiced for centuries and is still exceptionally relevant for today's distracted culture. You can practice Lectio Divina by yourself or with a group. One Lectio exercise includes four (or sometimes five) steps and will usually take about fifteen or twenty minutes.

THE STEPS OF LECTIO DIVINA

Prepare your heart, making it available. Be ready to listen. Lower the tone of the voices around you. Ask the Holy Spirit to accompany and guide you to perceive God's voice that speaks through the Scriptures.

1. READING *(Lectio).* **What does the text say?**

   Read through the Bible passage—slowly. Read out loud if you are part of a group, and maybe even if you are by yourself. Consider the people speaking or acting in the passage. Reflect on the time, place, feelings, actions, and senses involved. Write down what you discover. Leave room for silence after you finish reading the passage.

2. MEDITATION *(Meditatio).* **What does the text say to you?**

   Read through the passage slowly again. Focus on what strikes you personally in the passage. Explore what God is trying to show you through Scripture. Connect the text to your life circumstances and struggles.

3. PRAYER *(Oratio).* **How do you respond to the text?**

   Now that God has spoken to you through the Bible passage, you can respond to God in prayer. You can ask for forgiveness, give thanks, recite a memorized prayer, or write in a journal. You can also read a psalm or another suitable Bible passage as your prayer.

3

4. CONTEMPLATION *(Contemplatio).* **What can God teach you in silence?**

Lectio Divina incorporates silence in all its steps, but this step focuses on silence with more intention. Allow yourself to be embraced by God's presence. Sit quietly to take it all in—and listen for God's voice.

5. ACTION *(Actio).* **How can you apply God's Word to everyday life?**

Consider how what you experienced through reading, meditation, prayer, and contemplation might compel you to live differently today. What new practices can you incorporate into your life? How can you live out this experience in your community and public roles? Now is the time to put what you've learned into concrete action.

ABOUT THIS COLLECTION

This collection adapts a four-step approach to Lectio Divina. Each week's exercise combines READING with what might be called a STUDY step *(Studio)* to help you think about what the Bible passage says. The *Contemplatio* often includes both CONTEMPLATION and ACTION steps.

These Lectio are written for use by people from all traditions, including those new to the Bible. The readings follow the three-year cycle of the Roman Catholic Sunday Lectionary (the Revised Common Lectionary is nearly the same). Dates and Sunday observances vary slightly each time a cycle returns. This volume includes Lectio Divina written over two cycles of Year C (2019, 2022, 2025, 2028, 2031).

The reflections were written to be sent by email during the week before a Sunday observance. We also note the other Bible passages assigned for that Sunday so that readers may prepare for worship.

Each volume begins with the First Sunday of Advent. The titles are taken from Jesus's words in the opening Gospel for each year: *Stay Awake!* (Matthew, Year A); *Be Alert!* (Mark, Year B); *Be Vigilant!* (Luke, Year C). Each volume concludes with the Solemnity of our Lord Jesus Christ, King of the Universe. We hope you find comfort for your soul and prompting for your life as you meet this loving King and hear his voice in these pages.

Be Vigilant!

BE VIGILANT

LUKE 21:25-28, 34-36

[25] "There will be signs in the sun, the moon, and the stars, and on earth nations will be in dismay, perplexed by the roaring of the sea and the waves. [26] People will die of fright in anticipation of what is coming upon the world, for the powers of the heavens will be shaken. [27] And then they will see the Son of Man coming in a cloud with power and great glory. [28] But when these signs begin to happen, stand erect and raise your heads because your redemption is at hand."

[34] "Beware that your hearts do not become drowsy from carousing and drunkenness and the anxieties of daily life, and that day catch you by surprise [35] like a trap. For that day will assault everyone who lives on the face of the earth. [36] Be vigilant at all times and pray that you have the strength to escape the tribulations that are imminent and to stand before the Son of Man."

—————————————— *Lectio* ——————————————

This week the faithful prepare for the first Sunday of Advent and the start of a new church year focusing on the Gospel according to Luke. St. Luke was a Gentile who became a follower of Jesus through the ministry of St. Paul. He reminds those who read his Gospel that he has "carefully investigated everything from the beginning" so that he can present an orderly and authoritative account of Jesus and his public ministry (Luke 1:1-4). Luke is also the author of the book of Acts, the sequel to this Gospel. A full third of the New Testament is credited to this great saint of God.

In our reading this week we meet Jesus in the middle of his "apocalyptic discourse," which begins when Jesus boldly predicts that the temple will be torn down within the lifetime of those listening. Not a single stone will be left upon another. During this period Jerusalem's temple symbolized all Judaism. Beyond its identity as the sacrificial center and the very house of God, the temple also represented the financial and cultural strength of the Jewish people. To appreciate the emotional impact of its destruction, we would have to imagine that in a single day the world loses the New York Stock Exchange, the U.S. Capitol, the White House, Oxford and Cambridge Universities, and Vatican City along with St. Peter's Cathedral. The temple in the time of Jesus was all of this and more. His specific and shocking prophesy will be fulfilled in AD 70 when a Roman army under the command of General (and future Emperor) Titus breaches the city defenses and razes the temple. It is never rebuilt.

Here Jesus speaks of "signs in the sun, the moon, and the stars." Events on earth will cause general panic and dismay. People will "die of fright" because the powers of the heavens will be shaken. This kind of figurative language is common to the apocalyptic (from the Greek for "unveiling"), a genre meant to be heard and interpreted in a literary rather than a literal sense. The references to sun, moon, and stars, for example, point to political upheaval. Recall the wise men from the east—when a new star appeared in a constellation associated with the Jewish people, they read it as an indication of a new king and came to Jerusalem to pay homage.

When all of this comes to pass those listening that day will remember this prophecy and will recognize the Son of Man (a title of the Messiah that Jesus appropriates for himself) as a figure of great power and worthy of honor. The boldness of the prediction and the sheer unlikeliness of its ever being fulfilled will bring glory to the Son of Man, the Messiah and Savior of the world. But Jesus's disciples are not to not cower as they hear the news of the temple's destruction. They will lift up their heads in prayer and praise to God, acknowledging that they have heeded the warning of Jesus and are ready as a new order dawns.

—————————————————————— *Meditatio* ——————————————————————

Please take a moment this week to note that in the Gospel reading two personal responses to times of tribulation are imagined. The first is terror—people dying of fright as they anticipate what is coming upon the world. Their world, the ten provinces that made up the Roman Empire, may have felt smaller than ours. Still, the thought of armies advancing to lay siege on Jerusalem was enough to shake the Israelites' "heavens and earth."

The second response is faith. Jesus instructs the disciples that when they see this prophecy come to fulfillment they should, "stand erect and raise your heads because your redemption is at hand." The same earth-shaking events come to pass. One person responds in fear and another in faith. We want to be on the faith side of that equation.

Our world is larger than the Roman Empire, and we are also all too familiar with nations in dismay. We hear daily about wars and rumors of war, of earthquakes and volcanoes, of fires and other natural disasters. As believers we are blessed to be able to choose how we will respond. Every day we live is one day closer to our own end time, and one day closer to the end of the world. Let's do our best to live out each day as persons of faith, vigilant and prayerful at all times so that we, like the first generation who followed Jesus, can stand confidently before the Son of Man when he returns to judge the living and the dead—or when he calls us home. Whichever is first, come, Lord Jesus.

─────────── *Oratio* ───────────

This prayer is known as the "embolism" and is used after the Lord's Prayer in the liturgy. It is a good prayer to pray this week as we enter the season of Advent full of spiritual anticipation.

Deliver us, Lord, we pray, from every evil and graciously grant peace in our days, that, by the help of your mercy, we may be always free from sin and safe from all distress, as we await the blessed hope and the coming of our Savior, Jesus Christ.

─────────── *Contemplatio* ───────────

Jesus brings the apocalyptic discourse to an end with the admonition to be vigilant, sober, and alert. He warns us not to let our hearts become drowsy from "carousing and drunkenness and the anxieties of daily life." We can all recognize how often the "anxieties of life" interfere with our relationship with the Lord. Pray this week to find more spiritual clarity in your own walk of faith.

Advent is a season of anticipation, a season of expectation. Use the four short weeks of this liturgical season to your spiritual advantage. It is an excellent time to add, even in a small way, a spiritual practice or two to your week. Maybe it will be a fresh personal devotion, a spiritual book—newly purchased or dusted off from your shelves—to engage your mind with the things of God. How about trying to attend a Bible study or even daily Mass during these weeks? These sorts of activities will help you to stay awake, to stay sober and alert so that you will ready to respond to the needs of others in your community and beyond.

OTHER READINGS: JEREMIAH 33:14-16; 1 THESSALONIANS 3:12—4:2

SECOND SUNDAY OF ADVENT

THE WORD OF GOD CAME

LUKE 3:1-6

[1] In the fifteenth year of the reign of Tiberius Caesar, when Pontius Pilate was governor of Judea, and Herod was tetrarch of Galilee, and his brother Philip tetrarch of the region of Ituraea and Trachonitis, and Lysanias was tetrarch of Abilene, [2] during the high priesthood of Annas and Caiaphas, the word of God came to John the son of Zechariah in the desert. [3] He went throughout [the] whole region of the Jordan, proclaiming a baptism of repentance for the forgiveness of sins, [4] as it is written in the book of the words of the prophet Isaiah:

"A voice of one crying out in the desert:
'Prepare the way of the Lord,
  make straight his paths.
[5] Every valley shall be filled
  and every mountain and hill shall be made low.
The winding roads shall be made straight,
  and the rough ways made smooth,
[6] and all flesh shall see the salvation of God.'"

—— *Lectio* ——

In this, the second Sunday of Advent we return to the Gospel of Luke. We saw last week Luke's concern for careful investigation so that he can record the Jesus narrative for Theophilus in an orderly manner. His orderliness comes out clearly in the reading this week as he describes the well-attested ministry of John, known as "the Baptist."

Setting the historical stage, Luke lists six figures who hold civil and religious authority. The word of God comes to John, he says, in the fifteenth year of Tiberius Caesar, who will rule the Roman world as emperor until his death in AD 37. Luke then mentions Pontius Pilate, who represents Rome as prefect or governor of the province of Judea, subordinate to the larger province of Syria, and will serve in that capacity until AD 36. Herod and Philip are sons of Herod the Great. These local princes are called tetrarchs, a title indicating that they are subordinate to the rule of Pilate in their regions. Herod Antipas rules in Galilee until AD 39 and his brother Philip rules in Upper Galilee until AD 34. History doesn't record anything more of Lysanias; the territory of Abilene was northwest of Damascus.

Luke also mentions the names of the two high priests who served in the Jerusalem temple. This is unusual, because high priest was a hereditary position, and a new priest was anointed only after his predecessor's death. During the childhood of Jesus (the true High Priest) the high priest Annas had been deposed by Rome in AD 15 but still wields great influence. After going through a few other family members, Rome allowed the high priesthood to come to Caiaphas, the son-in-law of Annas. Caiaphas remains high priest until his demise in AD 36.

Luke wants his readers to know that all of these influencers were alive and active during the public ministry of both John the Baptist and Jesus. It is his way of anchoring his Gospel securely in history.

Now Luke can introduce his readers to John, the son of Zechariah. He states clearly that the word of God came to and through John to those who came to be dipped under the water of the Jordan River. Luke identifies John as a prophet, a person who speaks the words of God. This is an accolade of the highest honor. Later in the Gospel Jesus will refer to his cousin John as a prophet and so much more (Luke 7:26). John is a critical historical character in the story of salvation. He knows that he is the one the prophet Isaiah had in mind when he spoke about a herald, the voice of a man crying out in the wilderness who would arrive in advance of the Messiah to help others prepare the way for the Lord. As the Gospel moves forward Jesus will increase and John will not. Still, his call to turn around and prepare for the arrival of the Messiah paves the way for the appearance of Jesus and the beginning of his public ministry in Israel.

------------------------- *Meditatio* -------------------------

John appears on the eastern side of the Jordan River calling out to those who cross that they need to repent (literally, turn around and come back) so that they can be baptized (dipped) under the coursing waters of this river, so rich in biblical memory and miracle. The baptism by John was a way to show your desire to restore your relationship with God and others that might have been broken by sin.

The Bible defines sin as a condition of alienation and separation from God and others. We move away from God. God does not move away from us. This separation can be categorized in degrees of seriousness from simple acts of alienation to those more serious, and on to a final stage that imperils your mortal soul. When we repent our sin is forgiven and the debt incurred by sin is erased. We come back to a loving God. The Baptist's call to repent is an invitation to restored fellowship and communion with God and others in the community of faith.

John was a prophet of God whose voice was clarion and clear. Whose voice carries the same weight today in your life? In the life of your faith community? Advent is the perfect season to listen for that call to repentance and restoration. Use the weeks of Advent to prepare your way back to the Lord. Fill the valleys and lower the hills in your life. Make the winding ways straight so that your journey back will be easy and a witness to others about how much they too are loved by God.

------------------------- *Oratio* -------------------------

In the Lord's Prayer we ask the Lord to provide for us our daily bread, and for God to forgive our sins (presuming that we have forgiven those who have sinned against us). This theme of the forgiveness of sins is central to the message of John the Baptist. Pray the Our Father with the awareness that we are asking for forgiveness of sins as you anticipate hearing this Gospel proclaimed this weekend.

Luke tells us this week that the word of God came to John. In the Bible men and women who receive and proclaim God's word in the community are known as prophets. The role of prophet continues in the Christian church whenever a representative of the clergy leads worship and preaches the Word to assembled believers. Who is the prophet in your life? Who preaches the Word of God in your community? Hold that person in prayer. Ask the Father to speak boldly through their words and through the lives they live. The role of prophet is critical in the life of the church. Supporting those who speak in the name of the Lord is an important and timely response to the Gospel this week.

OTHER READINGS: BARUCH 5:1–9; PHILIPPIANS 1:4–6, 8–11

THIRD SUNDAY OF ADVENT

THE FRUITS OF EXPECTATION

LUKE 3:10-18

¹⁰ And the crowds asked him, "What then should we do?" ¹¹ He said to them in reply, "Whoever has two tunics should share with the person who has none. And whoever has food should do likewise." ¹² Even tax collectors came to be baptized and they said to him, "Teacher, what should we do?" ¹³ He answered them, "Stop collecting more than what is prescribed." ¹⁴ Soldiers also asked him, "And what is it that we should do?" He told them, "Do not practice extortion, do not falsely accuse anyone, and be satisfied with your wages."

¹⁵ Now the people were filled with expectation, and all were asking in their hearts whether John might be the Messiah. ¹⁶ John answered them all, saying, "I am baptizing you with water, but one mightier than I is coming. I am not worthy to loosen the thongs of his sandals. He will baptize you with the holy Spirit and fire. ¹⁷ His winnowing fan is in his hand to clear his threshing floor and to gather the wheat into his barn,

but the chaff he will burn with unquenchable fire." ¹⁸ Exhorting them in many other ways, he preached good news to the people.

═══════════════ *Lectio* ═══════════════

In the Gospel reading for the third Sunday in Advent we find John the Baptist on the eastern side of the Jordan River at the well-traveled fording point along the road leading through Jericho and into the hills beyond where their final destination, Jerusalem, awaits weary pilgrims. Men and women from all over the region arrive at this ford to see this desert prophet for themselves, and in the verses immediately before this week's passage, John has just insulted them.

The people are proud of their ancestry as Abraham's descendants, but John calls the assembled crowd a "brood of vipers" who should be preparing for the coming wrath of God rather than gawking at him. The phrase is even more scandalous in context. Not only are they venomous snakes—a danger to all who come in contact with them and ritually impure because they live in the dust God cursed in Genesis 3. John also says they are vipers' offspring. At the time, people believed desert vipers ate their way out of the womb, murdering their mothers in the process of birth. John pulls no punches when it comes to a well-timed insult! (The parallel passage in Matthew 3 limits this insult to "merely" the nation's religious authorities.)

Now John responds to questions from the crowds. He tells three distinct groups how they might be expected to reform their lives in response to their baptism. Baptism was to have a dual effect. You first expressed your desire to be reunited with God by dipping your body in the Jordan. That experience was to be followed by a concrete change of behavior that would show others that your life had been transformed.

John speaks first to the bulk of the crowd. How are they to live differently? Anyone who has two tunics (you only need one) or an abundance of food should share with those lacking either. The economics of the ancient world were based on scarcity. To have more than you need could mean someone else goes without, so share your blessings with others.

Second, John responds to questions from tax collectors—men likely in the employ of the region's chief tax collector, Zacchaeus, headquartered in the city of Jericho a few miles west of the ford. Everyone knew that tax collectors took an extra cut for themselves and lived quite well off the hard-earned funds of others. John tells those who are baptized to be content with their commission and not to inflate the amounts owed to Rome so that they could pocket the difference.

John even engages questions asked by soldiers. These are probably members of the temple guard posted here by King Herod to ensure the safety of pilgrims on their way to Jerusalem. Pilgrims travel to the holy city three times annually—with full purses. King Herod wants to keep that economic engine running smoothly. These soldiers would have been nominally Jewish. John instructs those newly baptized to stop the common practice of false accusation used to extort funds from the innocent, and to be content with their wages.

All this blunt talk leads to a heightened sense of expectation. Could John be the Messiah? John denies it at every turn. He assures everyone that he is only preparing a way for the coming true Messiah.

Meditatio

The ministry of John the Baptist has people brimming with expectation. We can feel the excitement when we consider how many people cross the Jordan to the baptismal site. Religious leaders, faith-filled pilgrims, tax collectors, soldiers—who have we left out? Even Jesus, as his own ministry begins, will appear before his cousin, his baptism a sign that must be fulfilled as the sinless one is "counted among the transgressors" (Isaiah 53:12).

John tells the crowds that expectation needs to result in repentance, and repentance must be demonstrated in fruit—in action. John is not afraid to give specific counsel to all who ask for advice on how to reform their lives. Think too of the rich young ruler who asks Jesus what he must do to inherit eternal life, and of the woman caught in adultery counseled by Jesus to go and sin no more.

This heightened spirit of expectation carries over into the realities of our lives. An encounter with God brings an expectation of change. We will desire to live a new way. In Jesus, the old is gone, and something new is born in us, something we need to find a way to express in action. That is the journey of Advent, this season of waiting and expectation. Now is the perfect time to examine our lives for evidence we have been changed.

We have been dipped under the waters of baptism in order to do the work the Lord has waiting for us to accomplish. What is the Lord asking of you this Advent? What expectations have risen within you these past three weeks? Listen and act on one of these inspirations.

Oratio

Our prayer response will focus on reforming our spiritual lives in both word and deed. Listen to the prophet Micah's summary of the will of God for our lives: "You have been told, O mortal, what is good, and what the LORD requires of you: Only to do justice and to love goodness, and to walk humbly with your God" (Micah 6:8).

Father, give me the desire I need to support works of justice on behalf of the poor, to choose the way of the good over the way of evil, and the courage to trust that a humble walk with you will bring the light of faith to a world darkened by sin. Amen.

Contemplatio

Deeds trump creeds. This spiritual gem was shared with me by my friend Rabbi Michael Mayershom, who has a unique ability to teach Christians about their Jewish roots in prayer and practice. The author of the letter of James has the same advice: "Indeed someone may say, 'You have faith but I have works.' Demonstrate your faith to me without works and I will demonstrate my faith to you from my works" (James 2:18). Expressing faith through action is the goal of the spiritual life.

Be open to opportunities that will allow you to put your faith into action during this Advent season. Be open to how the Spirit guides you to love and serve new populations with a new enthusiasm. We know what we believe, and now is the time to express that belief in action. God bless you.

OTHER READINGS: ZEPHANIAH 3:14–18a; PHILIPPIANS 4:4–7

REMARKABLE WOMEN

LUKE 1:39–45

³⁹ During those days Mary set out and traveled to the hill country in haste to a town of Judah, ⁴⁰ where she entered the house of Zechariah and greeted Elizabeth. ⁴¹ When Elizabeth heard Mary's greeting, the infant leaped in her womb, and Elizabeth, filled with the holy Spirit, ⁴² cried out in a loud voice and said, "Most blessed are you among women, and blessed is the fruit of your womb. ⁴³ And how does this happen to me, that the mother of my Lord should come to me? ⁴⁴ For at the moment the sound of your greeting reached my ears, the infant in my womb leaped for joy. ⁴⁵ Blessed are you who believed that what was spoken to you by the Lord would be fulfilled."

———————— *Lectio* ————————

Each Gospel story has a backstory. The context for this week's narrative includes two separate annunciation events, both recorded in the Gospel of Luke and both involving the two pregnant women who now greet one another in a small village outside Jerusalem. Mary the mother of Jesus greets her elder kinswoman Elizabeth. Each woman has received word through the archangel Gabriel that she will deliver a son with a role in salvation history. Elizabeth's son John will "prepare a people fit for the Lord" (Luke 1:17), heralding the coming Messiah, the son of Mary. These women—and the boys in their wombs—meet in our reading this week.

Mary may have been sent to Elizabeth in part to allow her fiancé Joseph time to sort out a proper response to the news that she was with child by the will and agency of God. Joseph needed to consider his options (including the possibility of a quiet divorce). A visit to her aging and pregnant cousin would be prudent. Mary's sudden departure can easily be explained in the village and the duration of her stay will be tied to the circumstances surrounding the birth of Elizabeth's child. In the three months Mary is away Joseph can seek counsel and pray about his next move.

No one travels alone in the biblical period, especially not women. Mary would have had company on the way. The journey from Nazareth to the village of Ein Karem—which tradition suggests was the home of Elizabeth and her husband Zechariah—is nearly one hundred miles and would take up to four days to complete. When she reaches her destination, Luke tells us that Mary "greeted" her kinswoman Elizabeth and the child Elizabeth carries in her womb "leaped for joy."

A Middle Eastern greeting like the one referred to in the Gospel involves a detailed exchange as both parties ask about all the circumstances of their meeting together. Such greetings take time! Recall that in Luke 10 Jesus has to instruct his missionary disciples not to greet anyone along the road as they make their way through the towns and villages of Galilee. If they stop to greet people in this long and involved Middle Eastern manner they will never arrive at their intended destinations!

This greeting allows the women to share their stories with each other. Clearly Mary tells her cousin about Gabriel's announcement of her pregnancy, and in the course of the story the growing child in Elizabeth's womb stirs, to the delight of both expectant mothers. Elizabeth concludes that Mary is going to be the holy vessel through whom God will send the Messiah. Elizabeth calls her "the mother of my Lord" for this very reason. Mary's greeting to Elizabeth is also the reason Elizabeth exclaims, "Most blessed are you among women, and blessed is the fruit of your womb."

———————————— *Meditatio* ————————————

We meet many remarkable women in the Gospel of Luke. This Gospel includes twenty-three unique stories about women. Without his perspective on women in the life and ministry of Jesus we would know little or nothing about three great women—Elizabeth the mother of John the Baptist; Mary the mother of Jesus the Messiah; and Anna the prophetess, who will meet Mary in the temple and confirm to her that what God has begun, God will complete with her son Jesus (Luke 2:36–38).

Luke also tells us of the women of means in Galilee who support Jesus's ministry (Luke 8:1–3). Martha and her sister Mary are numbered among his closest friends and called his disciples. And only the Gospel of Luke records Jesus's parables with additional engagement for women. Luke pairs the parable of the mustard seed with the parable of the leaven (breadmaking was women's work). The parable of lost sheep for the men is paired with the parable of the lost coin to challenge his female disciples.

Who are the spiritual women in your life? How do they reveal the Lord to you? Can you recall them by name? What role have they played in your growth as a Christian? Take a moment to thank God for the blessing that these women have been in your life. Ask God to impart a special blessing on each of them this week.

Oratio

The prayer Catholics call the Hail Mary is drawn from this week's passage in the Gospel of Luke. Let it be our prayer this week: "Hail Mary, full of grace, the Lord is with you. Blessed are you among women and blessed is the fruit of your womb, Jesus."

Contemplatio

Take a few moments this week to formulate your own "Middle Eastern" greeting like the one shared between Elizabeth and Mary. This greeting should include information about what God has been doing in your life and how you have been able to respond to God's call. Imagine a setting in which you could share this greeting as a testimony to God's grace, alive and active in you and your life. What details would you include? What has God been doing in you this Advent season? Where has there been spiritual growth in your life? How have you been challenged to step out in faith? Now ask the Lord to provide someone with whom you can share this sort of personal greeting, possibly during the coming season of Christmas. Be open and available to share your greeting when the time comes. And have a blessed celebration of Christmas!

OTHER READINGS: MICAH 5:1–4a; HEBREWS 10:5–10

THREE DAYS' SEARCH

LUKE 2:41–52

[41] Each year his parents went to Jerusalem for the feast of Passover, [42] and when he was twelve years old, they went up according to festival custom. [43] After they had completed its days, as they were returning, the boy Jesus remained behind in Jerusalem, but his parents did not know it. [44] Thinking that he was in the caravan, they journeyed for a day and looked for him among their relatives and acquaintances, [45] but not finding him, they returned to Jerusalem to look for him. [46] After three days they found him in the temple, sitting in the midst of the teachers, listening to them and asking them questions, [47] and all who heard him were astounded at his understanding and his answers. [48] When his parents saw him, they were astonished, and his mother said to him, "Son, why have you done this to us? Your father and I have been looking for you with great anxiety." [49] And he said to them, "Why were you looking for me? Did you not know that I must be in my Father's house?" [50] But they did not understand what he said to them. [51] He went down with them and came to Nazareth, and was obedient to them; and his mother kept all these things in her heart. [52] And Jesus advanced [in] wisdom and age and favor before God and man.

Lectio

The story of Jesus left behind at the temple is unique to Luke and is the only mention in any Gospel account of an event associated with his childhood. The source seems to have been his mother Mary and suggests that Luke was able to interview her as he wrote. The account opens by explaining that the parents of Jesus are devout Jews. Each year they have traveled the hundred miles from the village of Nazareth in Galilee to the holy city of Jerusalem. This was not typical of all families at the time. Jesus is a youth of twelve as they arrive to celebrate the seven-day Passover feast. When the festival is finished the family prepares to return to Nazareth. Mary and Joseph complete the first day-long journey, likely from Jerusalem to Jericho. Pilgrims would travel in separate groups—women, girls, and boys under twelve walking in front and the men and older boys coming behind.

It is culturally plausible that Mary does not worry that Jesus is not among her female companions that day. He has at last entered the exclusive world of the males and would travel in Joseph's company. Joseph may have looked for Jesus among the men preparing to travel with him to Jericho. Does he feel a pang of disappointment that Jesus is not with him? Jesus must still be traveling with the women this trip. Maybe next year.

Imagine the shock and fear when Joseph and Mary find one another in Jericho and realize Jesus is not with either of them. What has happened to their son? After a diligent search among their relatives and friends, Mary and Joseph take the long and winding road back to Jerusalem. The search will continue for nearly three days—with the possibility setting in that Jesus may never be found—before they come to the temple. They are amazed to find their son seated among the religious leaders on the temple mount. Jesus is amazing them with his thoughtful questions and his intelligent responses to their own challenging questions.

His mother speaks to Jesus on behalf of both parents. Jesus has until now been raised in the primary—perhaps even exclusive—care of the females of his village. His principal teacher would have been his mother, and he owed her absolute obedience. Her work will be complete when he officially enters the world of men in the next year or so. Mary asks Jesus, "Son, why have you done this to us?" Jesus is confident in his response. They should have known he had to be in his Father's house. They do not understand what this means.

Such a bold declaration that the temple is "my Father's house" would be considered blasphemous on the lips of anyone over the age of thirteen. The religious authorities make no such accusation against Jesus. He is given the benefit of doubt since he is still just a youth. That will change soon enough. Mary and Joseph collect Jesus. He returns to Nazareth and is obedient to them. In the years that follow Jesus will advance in "wisdom and age and favor before God and man" until his public ministry begins eighteen years later.

"Son, why have you done this to us? Your father and I have been looking for you with great anxiety." As a parent I can imagine the sense of dread Mary and Joseph must have felt as they begin their painstaking search for Jesus in Jericho. I have traveled that same ancient path to Jerusalem, well known as the setting of the parable of the Good Samaritan. In that parable, a Jewish man is attacked, beaten, robbed, and left for dead along this road, which had a well-deserved reputation for banditry. Mary and Joseph must have examined every ledge, every turn, every possible spot for mishap, hoping against hope that they would find Jesus alive.

What led them to the temple that third day? Had they given up hope? They had retraced their steps and still could not find their son. Was a direct appeal to God in the holy temple their final option? On the temple mount they find him, seated among the teachers. In the ancient world teachers are seated and students stand to listen. The fact that Jesus is seated indicates that he is being honored by these religious leaders and tells us much about the young boy's keen wit and spiritual insight.

What was the relief of Mary and Joseph like at that moment? Can you place yourself in the scene and imagine your own response? What emotions would parents experience on finally finding a child that they were sure was lost forever? Imagine the look, the embrace, and the emotional exchange in that moment before anyone speaks. Hold on to that moment in your meditation this week. Allow that image to transform your soul.

—————— *Oratio* ——————

Mary and Joseph prayed in earnest, asking God the Father to help them find their lost child. This reminds us of Jesus and his teaching about the importance of persistence in prayer. This week, bring the teaching in Matthew 7:7 (NLT) to your prayers: *"Keep on asking, and you will receive what you ask for. Keep on seeking, and you will find. Keep on knocking, and the door will be opened to you."*

No one asks only once. No one looks in just one place for a lost item. And no one knocks at a door a single time. You ask and keep on asking. You look and you keep on looking. You knock and you keep on knocking.

Be biblical in your prayer this week. Keep on asking, keep on seeking, and keep on knocking. Be ready for God to respond.

———————————— *Contemplatio* ————————————

At the of the reading we see that Mary treasured this event in her heart. Why do you think Luke shares this detail? I am convinced Mary is his eye-witness source. The early Christian churches maintained that Mary, given into the care of the apostle John by Jesus at his crucifixion (John 19:26–27) remained in John's care until the end of her days. John was ministering in Ephesus at roughly the time St. Paul and St. Luke arrived. I imagine Luke and Mary often having tea together over the two and half years of that visit, as Luke asks about her memories of Jesus as a man and as a child.

It seems that one memory she held dear was the relief she and Joseph felt in finally finding Jesus alive and well in the temple. This was the memory that she treasured in her heart. What is yours? What spiritual memory in your journey of faith do you recall with heartfelt fondness? If someone were to ask you so share such a memory this week what would it be? Take a few moments to dwell on these questions as you prepare to hear the Gospel again this weekend.

OTHER READINGS: 1 SAMUEL 1:20–22, 24–28; 1 JOHN 3:1–2, 21–24

THE EPIPHANY OF THE LORD

PROVIDENTIAL GIFTS

MATTHEW 2:1-12

[1] When Jesus was born in Bethlehem of Judea, in the days of King Herod, behold, magi from the east arrived in Jerusalem, [2] saying, "Where is the newborn king of the Jews? We saw his star at its rising and have come to do him homage." [3] When King Herod heard this, he was greatly troubled, and all Jerusalem with him. [4] Assembling all the chief priests and the scribes of the people, he inquired of them where the Messiah

was to be born. [5] They said to him, "In Bethlehem of Judea, for thus it has been written through the prophet:

> [6] 'And you, Bethlehem, land of Judah,
>   are by no means least among the rulers of Judah;
>   since from you shall come a ruler,
>   who is to shepherd my people Israel.'"

[7] Then Herod called the magi secretly and ascertained from them the time of the star's appearance. [8] He sent them to Bethlehem and said, "Go and search diligently for the child. When you have found him, bring me word, that I too may go and do him homage." [9] After their audience with the king they set out. And behold, the star that they had seen at its rising preceded them, until it came and stopped over the place where the child was. [10] They were overjoyed at seeing the star, [11] and on entering the house they saw the child with Mary his mother. They prostrated themselves and did him homage. Then they opened their treasures and offered him gifts of gold, frankincense, and myrrh. [12] And having been warned in a dream not to return to Herod, they departed for their country by another way.

Lectio

This week the church celebrates the feast of the Epiphany. We remember the wise men who arrive in Jerusalem and are directed to Bethlehem, where they honor the holy family with gifts appropriate to their caravan trade. This story is unique to Matthew and prepares the reader for the Great Commission at the conclusion of his Gospel when Jesus directs the disciples to go and make disciples of all the nations (Matthew 28:16–20). God's plan of salvation has always included the Gentiles. Our magi are from the "east" and from among "the nations." They are Gentiles who will participate in God's plan of salvation.

The magi arrive unexpectedly. Typical of the time period, groups of traders would travel together in caravans moving their goods from their home villages to Egypt's lucrative markets. This is the case with the wise men in our Gospel. This helps explain why King Herod and the rest of Jerusalem are "greatly troubled" by their appearance—and by their inquiry about a newborn Jewish king. The reaction could be due to the unusual detour of a caravan into the hill country of Judea and Jerusalem.

We typically think of only three wise men because of the three gifts they leave with Joseph and Mary in Bethlehem, but there were certainly more than three men in a caravan that had traveled for the better part of six months to arrive in Jerusalem. King Herod seems too concerned about the nature of their visit. He learns that their appearance has to do with portents in the sky that suggest a new ruler has been born, a likely threat to his throne. Herod is a puppet king, a half-Jewish interloper set up in power by Rome. Any rival must be eliminated as soon as possible!

The wise men tell the king they have seen a "star" rise in the east. This rising star was probably the light in the early morning sky of planets (Venus or Saturn and Jupiter) in close proximity to one another. Stars are stationary, while planets move across the heavens. This "star" rose in the constellation Leo, the Lion, which the magi associated with the Jewish people and the Lion of Judah. A star rising, or appearing, suggested to them the birth of a new king. The wise men plan a detour on their way to Egypt to locate the heir to the throne to offer him gifts. They are certainly shocked to learn that King Herod knows nothing about an heir and has to consult his own "magi" to ascertain what Jewish prophets had written about the birth of the Messiah. They report to the king that the Messiah will be born in Bethlehem. If he has been born, they will find him there.

The magi meet secretly with King Herod and soon suspect he has a nefarious plan for the newborn child. Secrecy leads to suspicion in the open-door world of the Middle East. Anything done behind closed doors is suspect at best. The wise men learn from Herod where the child can be found. They also note that he is far too interested in this child himself. Their suspicions about Herod are intact as they journey south to Bethlehem where they locate the holy family in a village home. They greet Joseph and Mary, sharing with them the details of their journey and prepare to leave after offering gifts befitting a newborn king. They must have been offered hospitality in the village because God speaks to them in a dream and warns them to avoid any association with Herod in the future, so they depart from Bethlehem and return home by another way.

Gold, frankincense, and myrrh. The three gifts that the magi present to Joseph and Mary and the infant Jesus are an expression of their homage to the newborn king of the Jewish people. Each gift is a precious commodity made even more valuable by its portability and value in the distant markets of Egypt. In fact, the gold we typically associate with the first of the three gifts presented to the Holy Family was not in the form of coin at all. It was a special "golden" incense used on the highest altars in Egypt. Frankincense and myrrh are also types of incense. All three are going to prove valuable to Joseph and Mary when they are directed by the angel Gabriel to flee to Egypt to avoid the wrath of King Herod, who will order the murder of Bethlehem's innocent boys. The wise men, agents of God's provision, have supplied the Holy Family with a valuable source of funding that they will need to journey to Egypt. There they will live as refugees until they hear the news that Herod has passed.

As you meditate on this Gospel encounter, imagine yourself in that house, with the characters all around you that same evening. Use the eyes of your mind to take in the scene. Listen for the excited knock on the door. How did the wise men speak to Joseph and Mary about the reason for their unexpected visit, and for how long? Did they invite the new parents outside to see the "star," that light in the night sky that had guided them to Bethlehem from ancient Persia? How did they find this small hamlet that night? They seem to know that Jesus is a special child. Watch as they bow down to honor him as a royal figure and give the best of their caravan goods in an act of homage and worship. Joseph and Mary could not at the time have known the value of those gifts and how providential they would be. Consider how God works in mysterious and wonderful ways.

Oratio

Psalm 19:1–5a helps capture the wonder of the magi in their joy at seeing the star rise in the east, of their journey to Jerusalem and the discovery of the child Jesus in Bethlehem. It will be our prayer of preparation this week.

"The heavens declare the glory of God; the firmament proclaims the works of his hands. Day unto day pours forth speech; night unto night whispers knowledge. There is no speech, no words; their voice is not heard; a report goes forth through all the earth, their messages, to the ends of the world."

—————————— *Contemplatio* ——————————

In the Eastern Orthodox Church the feast of Epiphany is the time to give gifts in memory of those given by the wise men. Start a new tradition among your family and friends this week. Purchase a special "epiphany" gift for someone and deliver this surprise as part of embracing the memory of the magi. Pray that the gift is received as an expression of your love and honor for the person who will receive your gift as a blessing. Pray that it might even be part of God's unexpected provision. Perhaps this tradition will catch on in your family for years to come.

OTHER READINGS: ISAIAH 60:1–6; EPHESIANS 3:2–3a, 5–6

THE BAPTISM OF THE LORD

WELL PLEASED

LUKE 3:15–16, 21–22

¹⁵ Now the people were filled with expectation, and all were asking in their hearts whether John might be the Messiah. ¹⁶ John answered them all, saying, "I am baptizing you with water, but one mightier than I is coming. I am not worthy to loosen the thongs of his sandals. He will baptize you with the holy Spirit and fire."

²¹ After all the people had been baptized and Jesus also had been baptized and was praying, heaven was opened ²² and the holy Spirit descended upon him in bodily form like a dove. And a voice came from heaven, "You are my beloved Son; with you I am well pleased."

—————————— *Lectio* ——————————

Jesus once said that "among those born of women there has been none greater than John" the Baptist (Matthew 11:11). We meet this intriguing prophet again along the eastern shoreline of the Jordan River where he spends his days dipping men and women beneath these moving waters. Most of those baptized by John would be on their way to Jerusalem to participate in religious observances that require a ritual cleansing. The numbers of pilgrims approaching this prophetic figure increase by the day. Is it any wonder that the crowd is abuzz? Should they put their hope in him to deliver them from Roman military occupation? But John denies that he is the Messiah.

John was born a Levite and could have chosen to follow in the footsteps of his father Zechariah and serve in the temple as a priest. He has chosen another path, which has led him into these desert regions. He tells the crowds that he is a prophet, a voice of one crying in the wilderness to prepare the way for the Lord's true anointed one.

Jesus arrives and wants to be baptized by John. But why did Jesus need to be baptized? Certainly not for forgiveness. He had committed no sin. He asks that John baptize him because it is "fitting for us to fulfill all righteousness" (Matthew 3:15). So what does that mean?

Water and new beginnings are related in the biblical narrative of salvation. In Genesis, dry land is extracted from the waters of the sea to make humankind a place to live. To cleanse the world of sin a great flood covered the world; when dry land appears once again, Noah and his family are given a chance to begin anew. The Israelites pass through the parted waters of the Red Sea on their way to receive a law from God that will teach them a new way of living as God's people in the world. And the Israelites pass dry-shod through the Jordan River on their way into the land of promise to begin new lives under God's care and direction. In each story, passing under (or through) moving waters announces an opportunity to be obedient and to begin again.

Jesus understands the significance of this Jewish memory when he "fulfills all righteousness" by allowing John to dip him under the waters of the Jordan. He is the true Israelite, the new Israelite. He will express to John and his disciples that this symbolic act expresses obedience and faith in God. It is time for something new to break forth in the world. Those present on that day are not disappointed. Suddenly the heavens open and something akin to a dove descends on Jesus as he submits to the work of the Baptist. What does all of this mean?

Meditatio

"You are my beloved Son; with you I am well pleased." These are the words heard by the crowd when Jesus comes up from the waters of his baptism. Let them focus our meditation this week. In biblical times it was impossible to determine biological paternity. It was the duty of a father to claim the newborn as belonging to him. This public claim would determine the future of the child as an heir in the family. These words come from heaven. God has spoken: Jesus is God's beloved Son. His willing obedience to be baptized is pleasing to the Father.

The power of affirmation is just as important today. I am the father of five grown children. They each know that I am "well pleased" with them because I tell them so all the time. They already know that I am their father and that I love them, but still they glow when they hear from me that I am delighted by their presence in my life and by the light that they are in the world. The power of affirmation is transformative. With whom are you "well pleased"? Let them know this week.

Oratio

After his baptism as Jesus is praying the heavens open and the Holy Spirit descends upon him in bodily form resembling a dove. We will imagine this scene as we pray together this week. "Come Holy Spirit, Come!"

Come Holy Spirit, and fill the hearts of your faithful and kindle in them the fire of your love. Send forth your Spirit and we shall be created and through us you shall renew the face of the earth.

Contemplatio

How did the baptism of Jesus "fulfill all righteousness"? From a Jewish perspective the act of ritual immersion proved Jesus's willingness to obey the Father, even if that meant taking a path that would ultimately lead to unimaginable suffering, a brutal death, and the grave. Passing under the waters of the Jordan was a symbolic way to say yes to the Father and the Father's plan of salvation.

Even before the end of the first century the baptism rite was a sign of initiation for new believers who professed their faith in Christ. They followed the example of Jesus and were dipped under the waters to indicate that they were also willing to follow wherever Jesus might lead. By the end of the first century the immersion experience took on additional theological meaning as a mirror of the passion of Jesus. When you went under the water you shared in the death of Jesus. Rising out of the water symbolized the resurrection and your commitment to begin a new life in Christ.

The baptism of Jesus is rich with symbolic meaning. The meaning can be appreciated anew as an adult if you were baptized as an infant. Take a few moments this week and ponder your own baptism. Take note of how the grace of the sacrament has moved you forward in your life of faith.

OTHER READINGS: ISAIAH 40:1–5, 9–11; TITUS 2:11–14; 3:4–7

SECOND SUNDAY IN ORDINARY TIME

THE NEW MOSES

JOHN 2:1-11

[1] On the third day there was a wedding in Cana in Galilee, and the mother of Jesus was there. [2] Jesus and his disciples were also invited to the wedding. [3] When the wine ran short, the mother of Jesus said to him, "They have no wine." [4] [And] Jesus said to her, "Woman, how does your concern affect me? My hour has not yet come." [5] His mother said to the servers, "Do whatever he tells you." [6] Now there were six stone water jars there for Jewish ceremonial washings, each holding twenty to thirty gallons. [7] Jesus told them, "Fill the jars with water." So they filled them to the brim. [8] Then he told them, "Draw some out now and take it to the headwaiter." So they took it. [9] And when the headwaiter tasted the water that had become wine, without knowing where it came from (although the servers who had drawn the water knew), the headwaiter called the bridegroom [10] and said to him, "Everyone

serves good wine first, and then when people have drunk freely, an inferior one; but you have kept the good wine until now." [11] Jesus did this as the beginning of his signs in Cana in Galilee and so revealed his glory, and his disciples began to believe in him.

--- *Lectio* ---

In our reading this week, Jesus performs the first of seven miraculous "signs" recorded in the Gospel of John. This first sign takes place in a village called Cana, at the base of the rocky ridge on which Nazareth sits. Cana is much larger than remote Nazareth, where Jesus has lived since around the age of seven.

Jesus and his disciples arrive on the "third" day, excited to participate in wedding festivities. Many Jewish weddings are celebrated on this day of the week, a reference to the Genesis creation account. The work God completes on the third day is called "good" twice (Genesis 1:10, 12). As the only day that receives this double blessing, it was known as the best day of the week to marry. The first day of the week is Sunday, and in the Jewish lunar calendar the new day begins at sundown. Jesus and others traveling to Galilee arrive in Cana on Monday evening for the beginning of a seven-night reception to celebrate the marriage. Rabbis in Jesus's time taught that people should celebrate the union of a newly married couple for the same amount of time it took God to create the world.

Cana is located between the Mediterranean Sea and the Jezreel plain, geography perfectly suited to the cultivation of grapes. It had a regional reputation for producing the best local wine—the Napa or Sonoma of its day. Like anyone attending a destination wedding in Northern California, those who came to celebrate with the family would arrive expecting to be served the finest wine they had ever tasted. Upon arriving, Jesus meets his mother in the kitchen where she has been serving the host family. She informs Jesus that the family has run out of wine. This is a cause of great embarrassment to their loved ones and his mother's only request is that Jesus do something to rectify the situation.

Jesus's response seems terse, almost dismissive. He calls his mother "woman" and asks her what this situation has to do with him. First, the term "woman" in this context is not pejorative or even negative. It translates to "my dear one" and is a term of respect (though not commonly used with one's mother). Jesus will use the same term to address his sorrowful mother at the foot of the cross. Second, it seems that Jesus has previously discussed with his mother when his public ministry will begin—and that discussion did not involve solving a personal problem for some family friends. Jesus, however, always the obedient son, will do what his mother asks. She directs the servants to do whatever he tells them to do.

The six stone jars, when full, could hold over 120 gallons. That much water was needed for the ceremonial washing of so many guests—the same guests who have in a single day already consumed wine reserved for a week! Jesus orders the jars filled again. Servants complete the assigned task. They will be the first ones to witness a miracle of transformation. The water they fill the stone jars with is now wine.

Jesus directs these same servants to take a sample to the headwaiter, who would have been familiar with the best of the local vintage. He is amazed when he tastes it. Such wine should be held in reserve, not used to slake the never-ending thirst of these guests! Where had such a vintage been found? He questions the groom, obviously a young man without a great deal of wisdom. The best wine is presented to the guests first, just after they arrive, and then a lesser vintage later.

What will happen next? We don't know. The superior vintage is served. Jesus's mother is proud. The servants are impressed. His disciples wonder what this might mean. John tells us this is just the beginning of Jesus's public signs. Each successive sign will demand a response of faith from those who witness (and participate in) each miracle.

—— *Meditatio* ——

What is the significance of this being Jesus's first public miracle? Why would his disciples begin to believe in him as a result of what they see, taste, and hear? They are Jewish men and women of faith. They know the promise made by Moses in Deuteronomy 18:15 that one day another Prophet, one like himself, will arise in Israel, a Prophet who will do even more than Moses.

John shows how Jesus reveals himself as this new Moses in his first public sign, transforming fresh water into the best red wine. Recall that the first public miracle of Moses in Exodus 7 is when he calls down a curse on the life-giving waters of the Nile, transforming them into a foul and blood-red liquid. With his first public miracle Jesus surpasses Moses. Jesus transforms the refreshing waters of Cana's well into the best red wine any have ever tasted.

The source of the water in Cana still exists, still as clean, clear, and refreshing as it was in the time of Jesus. Moses prayed and the fresh waters of the Nile became foul. Jesus prayed and the best waters of Cana were suddenly made into wine. It was delicious—you tasted it and wanted more! In the minds of these earliest disciples, Jesus has bested Moses. Could he be the promised Messiah? This is the first sign. There will be more. They will have to wait and see—and so will you and I.

===================== *Oratio* =====================

A miracle of transformation. Jesus transforms water to the best wine the guests have ever tasted. This is the kind of transformation that we can pray for in our lives as well: *Lord, you are the God of transformations. Take the water that is my life and transform it into the good wine that will surprise and bless all those with whom I come in contact this week. Amen*

===================== *Contemplatio* =====================

Mary and Jesus must have been well known to the family hosting a seven-day wedding reception for their son. She is serving in their kitchen and keenly aware of their needs. She presses Jesus into service and he complies. What lesson can we learn from this engaging encounter?

Family is of paramount importance in the Middle East. At times it seems less so in our Western world. Pray for a chance to intercede and serve members of your own family and community. There is always someone in need. Follow the prompting of the Holy Spirit and act. Find a way to bless and assist another this week. The mother of Jesus told the servants to do whatever he told them to do. We should be willing to do the same.

OTHER READINGS: ISAIAH 62:1–5; 1 CORINTHIANS 12:4–11

FULFILLED IN YOUR HEARING

LUKE 1:1-4; 4:14-21

¹ Since many have undertaken to compile a narrative of the events that have been fulfilled among us, ² just as those who were eyewitnesses from the beginning and ministers of the word have handed them down to us, ³ I too have decided, after investigating everything accurately anew, to write it down in an orderly sequence for you, most excellent Theophilus, ⁴ so that you may realize the certainty of the teachings you have received.

4 ¹⁴ Jesus returned to Galilee in the power of the Spirit, and news of him spread throughout the whole region. ¹⁵ He taught in their synagogues and was praised by all.

¹⁶ He came to Nazareth, where he had grown up, and went according to his custom into the synagogue on the sabbath day. He stood up to read ¹⁷ and was handed a scroll of the prophet Isaiah. He unrolled the scroll and found the passage where it was written:

> ¹⁸ "The Spirit of the Lord is upon me,
>   because he has anointed me
>   to bring glad tidings to the poor.
> He has sent me to proclaim liberty to captives
>   and recovery of sight to the blind,
>   to let the oppressed go free,
> ¹⁹ and to proclaim a year acceptable to the Lord."

²⁰ Rolling up the scroll, he handed it back to the attendant and sat down, and the eyes of all in the synagogue looked intently at him. ²¹ He said to them, "Today this scripture passage is fulfilled in your hearing."

Lectio

This week the Gospel is sourced from two different chapters in Luke. First is the prologue, where we learn about the intention of our author, St. Luke, to write an orderly account of the life of Jesus. He informs his readers that he has "carefully investigated" the life of Jesus and has access to eye-witnesses who provide unique insight into events in the Lord's life that are not included in the earlier Gospels according to Matthew and Mark.

The readings now take the reader to Nazareth, a village situated high on a ridge overlooking the Jezreel valley and the boyhood home of Jesus. Jesus had been living here for at least twenty years, together with Mary his mother and his adoptive father Joseph, and would have been well known. He has been away for a while. Now he returns to Nazareth and attends the local synagogue, as was his weekly custom. He is recognized by the synagogue official and is invited to read and comment on a passage of his choice from the prophet Isaiah. This invitation to read and comment is an honor and reveals that Jesus is held in high regard among the villagers.

The scene is set for a drama to unfold. The prophecy of Isaiah fills a large scroll. (The copy of the book of Isaiah discovered among the scrolls kept by the Essene community who lived along the shores of the Dead Sea, measures thirty-six feet!) Scolls of the entire Bible were reverently stored in the synagogue tabernacle. When the attendant presents this scroll to Jesus, he honors the sacred text by standing to read.

The people wait as Jesus takes the time to unroll the scroll nearly to the end to find the portion he wants to read. When he finishes reading he carefully rolls up three dozen feet of parchment before handing it back to the attendant. Then he sits down. Teachers in the Middle East sit when they teach. Students stand in as close a proximity to the teacher as possible. They lean in to make sure they will hear every word that Jesus has to say. The eyes of everyone in the synagogue are fixed on him. Why? What has he done to elicit this intensity among those who know him so well? We have to wait until next week to find out the rest of the story!

—————————————— *Meditatio* ——————————————

The books of the Hebrew Bible are now read systematically in weekly synagogue gatherings. In the time of Jesus, the reader was free to choose any passage, a high honor. Jesus chooses a passage from Isaiah 61 that would have been familiar to those in attendance that day. He reads the first four verses of a longer poetic prophecy. When you read the first verses of a passage, the intention is to invoke the entire text in the memory of your listeners. We do this in our own culture when we hear a phrase like "fourscore and seven years ago." We know it as the opening line of the Gettysburg Address and thus know that the context of the quotation will relate to President Lincoln's speech. Jesus uses the same technique. He reads these four verses, likely with a particular vocal emphasis that *he* is the one anointed by God who is sent "proclaim liberty to the captives and recovery of sight to the blind, to let the oppressed go free ..." (NRSV).

Imagine yourself in the synagogue that day. You grew up with Jesus. You know Jesus and his family. You and your relatives and friends have for two decades gathered with them on Saturdays to pray. This day he is accorded the honor of reading from the sacred text and he seems to be insinuating that he is God's chosen agent, God's anointed, the Messiah of Israel! How can this be? Can he be serious?

Imagine Jesus reading the text with this self-referential emphasis. Where is this going to go? What will Jesus have to say about this reading? Watch as the scroll is slowly rolled up and returned to the attendant. Jesus sits in preparation to teach. Your eyes are fixed on Jesus as he says: "Today this scripture has been fulfilled in your hearing." That's right. That's what you heard. Their friend and neighbor has returned to Nazareth and he thinks he is the Messiah. The fireworks are ready to begin.

Oratio

Jesus chooses to read a passage from Isaiah. The message of the text is that when Messiah comes, he will bring recovery of sight to the blind.

Lord, send your Spirit upon me this week. Open my eyes so that I can see what you see this week. Give me the insight I need to be and act as your servant.

Contemplatio

Luke tells us that it was Jesus's custom to attend synagogue services every week. We have the same opportunity. Christians gather on Sunday to remember and celebrate the day of the Resurrection. Just like our Jewish ancestors in faith, Christians gather each week to hear the Word of God proclaimed and preached. This is what happens in the synagogue in Nazareth and continues in synagogues to this day.

God wants to speak to you this week. One of the best places this can happen is in church. When we show up and make attendance at church our custom, we allow the Holy Spirit the opportunity to speak to us anew. Our church experience, like the synagogue experience in New Testament times, is a place where we reconnect with God.

When Jesus finishes reading the portion from the prophet Isaiah all the eyes of the synagogue are fixed on him. There is a palpable sense of excitement and expectation. Pray for your pastor this week in anticipation of hearing the Word of God read and explained in your church. Ask the Holy Spirit to build a heightened sense of expectation and excitement for you and your community of faith.

OTHER READINGS: NEHEMIAH 8:2–4a, 5–6, 8–10; 1 CORINTHIANS 12:12–30

FOURTH SUNDAY IN ORDINARY TIME

GRACIOUS WORDS?

LUKE 4:21–30

²¹ He said to them, "Today this scripture passage is fulfilled in your hearing." ²² And all spoke highly of him and were amazed at the gracious words that came from his mouth. They also asked, "Isn't this the son of Joseph?" ²³ He said to them, "Surely you will quote me this proverb, 'Physician, cure yourself,' and say, 'Do here in your native place the things that we heard were done in Capernaum.'" ²⁴ And he said, "Amen, I say to you, no prophet is accepted in his own native place. ²⁵ Indeed, I tell you, there were many widows in Israel in the days of Elijah when the sky was closed for three and a half years and a severe famine spread over the entire land. ²⁶ It was to none of these that Elijah was sent, but only to a widow in Zarephath in the land of Sidon. ²⁷ Again, there were many lepers in Israel during the time of Elisha the prophet; yet not one of them was cleansed, but only Naaman the Syrian." ²⁸ When

the people in the synagogue heard this, they were all filled with fury. [29] They rose up, drove him out of the town, and led him to the brow of the hill on which their town had been built, to hurl him down headlong. [30] But he passed through the midst of them and went away.

─────── *Lectio* ───────

The Gospel opens where we left off last week. Jesus is in the synagogue of his hometown, Nazareth. He has been honored by being invited to read and comment on a portion of the Bible. The opening of his sermon shocks everyone: "Today this scripture is fulfilled in your hearing." How could that possibly be? Is Jesus claiming that he himself is the promised Messiah of Isaiah 61? Did we hear him say that the Spirit of the Lord is upon *him* to liberate captives, restore sight to the blind, and release others from oppression? They know Jesus; they know his father. He is the son of Joseph. Joseph is a *teknon*—the equivalent of a general contractor. Like father, like son. How can Jesus claim to be more than what Joseph brought him up to be? The congregation is growing more agitated by the minute.

We learn that everyone in the synagogue "spoke well of him" and are amazed at the "gracious words" that come from his mouth (verse 22), yet a few moments later these same people rise up in fury intending to drive Jesus off the nearby precipice to certain death. What are we missing here?

Jesus makes clear that he thinks he is the Messiah. Anyone in the synagogue that day would hear this claim as blasphemy. When we look at the congregation's response from this perspective the true meaning is revealed. Baptist biblical scholar David Biven once translated the Greek of the Gospel of Luke into biblical Hebrew and then back into modern English. (Hebrew and Aramaic were the two languages spoken by Jesus.) Dr. Biven translates their amazement in this verse this way: "everyone testified against him (they knew him well), being shocked at the words of his preaching." They can't believe what they are hearing from a person they thought they knew so well. This shock is what leads to the violent response. And Jesus is just getting warmed up!

The villagers know that Jesus had performed miracles elsewhere (nearby Cana comes to mind) before his return to Nazareth. Now Jesus reminds them that a prophet is never accepted in his own village. Even Elijah and Elisha—among the most famous prophets in the Hebrew Bible—performed miraculous interventions for Gentiles when they were not accepted by their own people. It is the final straw! Not only is Jesus claiming to be the Messiah, now he suggests that Messiah (like Elijah and Elisha before him) will find solace in serving Gentiles and not Jews.

Family comes first in the Middle East. What happened to family honor and loyalty to your home village? Tempers flare and bodily harm is threatened before Jesus heeds their warning and leaves Nazareth for good. The drama ends. The larger town of Capernaum, the home of disciples Peter and Andrew, will become his ministry headquarters from now on.

Meditatio

Jesus chooses to read a passage from the prophet Isaiah that revealed that Messiah will have a heart for those who are oppressed, for those who find themselves captive to man or to sin. When Messiah appears the poor will rejoice with rich blessings, the captured will be set free, the blind will see, and others will be released from their oppressions. It will be a year of favor. It will be a time that pleases God and will be known as a "year acceptable to the Lord." Messiah will seek out and serve the least before the mighty— and in the examples of Elijah and Elisha, the Gentiles before the Jews.

Who are the poor, blind, and oppressed in your life? How can you bless them this week? Do you know anyone who you can set free through forgiveness? Canceling a debt? Is anyone blind? Spiritually? What can you do to help them see? God is looking for the lowly and outcast through the prophets and through Jesus as Messiah. As his disciples, we have to be willing to do the same.

Oratio

The first half of the Prayer of St. Francis will be our response to the Gospel this week. It is our petition that God will make us men and women who will proclaim a year that is acceptable to the Lord. *"Lord make me an instrument of your peace. Where there is hatred let me sow love. Where there is injury, pardon. Where there is doubt, faith. Where there is despair, hope. Where there is darkness, light. And where there is sadness, joy."*

They thought they knew Jesus. He was the son of Joseph and had lived in their village for nearly his entire life. He had worked in his father's trade and become a respected member of the community. He always had some interesting insight to share after he read from the sacred text in synagogue. But this time it was different. The message shocked them; his insights infuriated them. They were out for blood. What would it take for you to have the same sort of emotionally charged response? How many sermons have we heard that simply encourage good people to keep being good? So many messages lack passion and fire. They don't inspire.

Pray for your minister this week. Take time to ask God's best for that person, and that they will have the courage and dedication to preach the whole message of the gospel. Pray that the words of the Gospel will come alive in a way that will amaze all who gather to worship with you this week. Come Holy Spirit! Enkindle in your ministers the fire of your love and bless them with the ability to rekindle the flame of faith in us all!

OTHER READINGS: JEREMIAH 1:4–5, 17–19; 1 CORINTHIANS 12:31—13:13

FIFTH SUNDAY IN ORDINARY TIME

SKILLS AND SECURITY

LUKE 5:1-11

[1] While the crowd was pressing in on Jesus and listening to the word of God, he was standing by the Lake of Gennesaret. [2] He saw two boats there alongside the lake; the fishermen had disembarked and were washing their nets. [3] Getting into one of the boats, the one belonging to Simon, he asked him to put out a short distance from the shore. Then he sat down and taught the crowds from the boat. [4] After he had finished speaking, he said to Simon, "Put out into deep water and lower your nets for a catch." [5] Simon said in reply, "Master, we have worked hard all night and have caught nothing, but at your command I will lower the nets." [6] When they had done this, they caught a great number

of fish and their nets were tearing. ⁷ They signaled to their partners in the other boat to come to help them. They came and filled both boats so that they were in danger of sinking. ⁸ When Simon Peter saw this, he fell at the knees of Jesus and said, "Depart from me, Lord, for I am a sinful man." ⁹ For astonishment at the catch of fish they had made seized him and all those with him, ¹⁰ and likewise James and John, the sons of Zebedee, who were partners of Simon. Jesus said to Simon, "Do not be afraid; from now on you will be catching men." ¹¹ When they brought their boats to the shore, they left everything and followed him.

—————————— *Lectio* ——————————

The reading opens with Jesus on the shore of Lake Gennesaret. This is the Sea of Galilee or the Sea of Tiberias—interchangeable names for this body of fresh water. The local fishermen have returned from their nightly catch. They work after dark because after sundown the marketable fish move from the lake's deep center into the shallows to chase shoals of bait fish. The fishermen hang lanterns over the sides of their vessels. The light attracts the bait fish, the bait fish attract the market fish, and the market fish attract commercial fishermen like Peter, Andrew, James, and John.

The fishermen are "washing" their nets. This seems an odd chore since the nets have presumably been in the water most of the night. In this case, the men are more "tending" the nets. They use gill nets made of fine twine that is easily broken by thrashing fish, so they spend the morning checking knots and mending tears in preparation for the next evening's outing.

The crowd on shore is getting larger by the minute. Jesus asks Peter if he will put his boat out a short distance from shore and steady the vessel with his careful attention to the oars. Jesus can now sit and teach the crowd amassed at the water's edge. Peter agrees. His work "day" is over. It has been a long night with nothing to show for his effort. Finishing his teaching, Jesus issues Peter a fishing-specific challenge. He invites him to row the boat out to deep waters and drop the nets for a catch.

At first glance Peter seems to honor Jesus in his response: "Master, we have worked hard all night and have caught nothing, but at your command I will lower the nets." But he knows he will catch no fish. The water is too deep. The fish are now on the bottom at a depth his nets could never reach. Still, he plays along. He does what Jesus asks and is shocked to feel the nets fill. The catch is so large he needs help to bring it in. Peter has to signal his partners to assist him with the valuable haul that fills two boats to the point of sinking!

Peter is astonished and tries to dismiss Jesus so he can get to work. That's right. In saying, "depart from me, Lord, for I am a sinful man," Peter is really trying to say to Jesus, "Thanks for the help, but I've got this now." Is he focusing on the task at hand so he won't be overwhelmed by considering the miracle? Still, these fish are valuable and need to be readied for market. And the commercial fisherman in him recognizes a new fishing area to which he can return again and again.

Jesus has Peter where he wants him. Now he invites Peter to leave all this security behind and follow him. It is time. What will Peter do? What would you do?

Meditatio

I am an avid fly fisherman and can easily enter into the mindset of Peter and his partners that day. After a long and fruitless night, Peter's mind wanders as he sits quietly in the boat, gently adjusting the oars so Jesus can speak freely to the crowds. It is not easy to hold a boat still, especially when a teacher of Jesus's caliber gesticulates to emphasize each point. Was he going over the previous evening's outing? What had he done wrong? Would the fishing be better tonight?

Jesus jars Peter out of his daydream. Put out into the deep water and let down the nets. Peter calls Jesus "Master," but he means something along the lines of, "Sure, Boss, I'll get right on that. That's a good plan that I am sure will bear fruit." He will show Jesus a thing or two about fishing now. If he caught nothing all night, there's no chance of catching anything in the bright light of morning. Jesus is from that ridgetop village of Nazareth. He may know a thing or two about building and grapevines, but not about fishing in waters Peter has known his whole life. And then the astonishment of the huge catch. Peter's mood changes dramatically that morning. He tries to dismiss Jesus but Jesus will have none of it. Bring the catch to shore and turn it over to your father. Jesus tells Peter it is time to leave all this behind with the confidence that Jesus will make him a fisher of men.

What would it take for you to leave behind what you love? What you do well? What you do to provide for your family? What miracle has Jesus done for you that cleared the way for you to follow him? That can be our meditation this week.

Oratio

I found this prayer on the prayray.com website. It is a prayer that God will make us all fishers in the kingdom: *Father God, we want the hands of the true fisher of men. Lord, help us to not be afraid to go wherever the fish are. Let us not be afraid to get our hands dirty. Father help us not to just "catch and release" new converts, let us also be disciplers of people as well. Amen.*

Contemplatio

Astonishment and surprise intrigue me this week. Jesus has been living in the home of Peter and his family for the better part of six months before he invites him to become a disciple. I have visited Capernaum many times and can tell you Peter would have made a good living. Peter's house is perfectly situated on the shore—prime real estate for a commercial fisherman. He has a successful business with partners and others in his employ.

Then he meets Jesus. Jesus and his mother Mary are welcomed as guests in Peter's sprawling family compound. Jesus honors his skill on the water. Jesus knows Peter well before he issues his invitation to discipleship. Jesus out-fishes a professional. Peter is "hooked" and leaves his nets behind to begin the process of becoming a fisher of men.

Jesus wants to use what we know and love and then call us into a deeper relationship through that gift or talent. Give some thought this week to what you know, what you are good at, and see if the Lord could use that love or skill to draw you closer to him. Take a few moments to ponder what Jesus knew about you before he invited you to become a "fisher of men" (and women) like Peter. Now that his net has found us, pray with me that he will use our talents and interests to draw in others to the kingdom.

OTHER READINGS: ISAIAH 6:1–2a, 3–8; 1 CORINTHIANS 15:1–11

LEAP FOR JOY!

LUKE 6:17, 20–26

[17] And he came down with them and stood on a stretch of level ground. A great crowd of his disciples and a large number of the people from all Judea and Jerusalem and the coastal region of Tyre and Sidon came to hear him …

[20] And raising his eyes toward his disciples he said:

> "Blessed are you who are poor,
>   for the kingdom of God is yours.
> [21] Blessed are you who are now hungry,
>   for you will be satisfied.
> Blessed are you who are now weeping,
>   for you will laugh.
> [22] Blessed are you when people hate you,
>   and when they exclude and insult you,
>   and denounce your name as evil
>   on account of the Son of Man.

[23] Rejoice and leap for joy on that day! Behold, your reward will be great in heaven. For their ancestors treated the prophets in the same way.

> [24] But woe to you who are rich,
>   for you have received your consolation.
> [25] But woe to you who are filled now,
>   for you will be hungry.
> Woe to you who laugh now,
>   for you will grieve and weep.
> [26] Woe to you when all speak well of you,
>   for their ancestors treated the false prophets in this way."

In the Gospel reading this week Jesus continues his public ministry in and around Galilee. Jesus has found a stretch of level ground, perhaps along the shoreline of the Sea of Galilee, where a large crowd of people have gathered. Anticipation is high. People have traveled here from as far away as Tyre in Sidon (along the coast of modern-day Lebanon) and also from the holy city of Jerusalem some ninety miles to the south. The crowd has been drawn to Jesus the healer. People are trying to touch him so his healing power might be imparted to them. Jesus is ready to speak and the eyes and ears of all are fastened on him.

There is a method to Jesus's public ministry, a threefold plan that draws large crowds of people to be challenged and transformed. Healings bring ever-larger crowds, seeking wholeness for themselves or for others. Once the healing is completed, Jesus turns to preaching to capture the attention and hearts of the listening audience. A great example of his preaching is revealed in the "level place" beatitudes that make up the bulk of our Gospel this week. Then Jesus reveals himself as a master teacher who continues to challenge and engage a now-captive audience. Healing, preaching, and then teaching. In that order. It works every time. This week we see Jesus the healer and preacher at his best.

The "level place" beatitudes in the Gospel of Luke differ slightly from the Sermon on the Mount beatitudes in Matthew 5. This is his "A-List" material that he expertly adapts to different audiences. The differences between our Lukan beatitudes and those in Matthew come because Jesus is preaching in two different locations to two different crowds. At this level place Jesus is among the poor, the hungry, and the oppressed. They are not the "poor in spirit" he engages in the Sermon on the Mount. These people have little in life to bring them joy. Jesus tells them that they also are blessed, that they are honored by God who sees their plight and will come to their assistance.

Jesus the preacher states boldly that if you are his disciple others will hate you. They will detach themselves from you and exclude you. They will insult you, denouncing your name as evil on account of the Son of Man, the title from Daniel 7:13–14 that Jesus claims for himself. He thus reveals himself as the promised Messiah to those who suffer at the hands of the rich and of well-fed, carefree overlords. He is *that* Son of Man. Jesus invites those listening to "Rejoice and leap for joy …" He is the promised Messiah who will right all wrongs and restore God's justice in the world.

───── *Meditatio* ─────

As I sat with this Gospel passage this week I was encouraged to reflect on the best "method" to share my faith with others. Bishop Robert Barron provides a helpful insight that fits with this week's meditation. He notes that the essential message of salvation is the proclamation of the goodness, truth, *and* beauty of the gospel message and of the church. He suggests that problems surface when we lead with the goodness of the message or the truthfulness of the message. We should be leading with the beauty of the invitation to follow Jesus. Jesus demonstrates his method in our reading this week. Miraculous healings are followed by inspiring words of preaching that he later codifies into specific teaching.

The hearer won't get to the teaching until you have first offered healing and the inspiration of heart that has been stirred to flame by the Spirit and the words of a great preacher. Jesus followed this method over the course of his public ministry, and his disciples copied his approach to great effect.

The same holds true as we think about goodness, truth, and beauty. It is difficult to lead someone to faith by sharing our ideas of "goodness." It is hard to gain someone's attention with, "Hey, I know what's good for you!" The response will rarely be positive. And don't expect a good response if you start with, "Hey, I know the truth and I want to share it with you." But what if we were to say, "Hey, do you want to see something beautiful?" Who could resist? Beauty is compelling. Let's learn to lead with what is beautiful about our faith. Meditate on what that might be for you, and be ready to share it this week.

───── *Oratio* ─────

Lord, send me the grace of trust, so that I can trust you in the midst of all of the challenges I face. When I feel poor, hungry, oppressed, or ostracized by others, send your Spirit to comfort and console me so that I can rejoice in you.

Jesus uses each beatitude in an effort to engage the hearts of the crowd that day. He expertly introduces a series of challenging statements to draw people of differing backgrounds and experiences into discipleship to him. He is recruiting new students on the fly. The crowd that day includes men and women who are abjectly poor, hungry, oppressed, and excluded by society. They hear that there is a place for them in the kingdom of God! They are blessed! They are honored! Jesus invites them to respond to the message and be transformed.

How do you respond to these beatitudes? Do you ever find yourself poor? Hungry? Oppressed? Rejected? If so, you are in good company. You are blessed too, and you can lean into Jesus. He is the Son of Man. He is the Messiah. He is the Lord and the Savior. These are wonderful reasons to rejoice and leap for joy. Leaping for joy? I'll bet you haven't done that in a while. Give it a try this week—but be careful!

OTHER READINGS: JEREMIAH 17:5–8; 1 CORINTHIANS 15:12, 16–20

SEVENTH SUNDAY IN ORDINARY TIME

HIGH CALLINGS

LUKE 6:27-38

[27] "But to you who hear I say, love your enemies, do good to those who hate you, [28] bless those who curse you, pray for those who mistreat you. [29] To the person who strikes you on one cheek, offer the other one as well, and from the person who takes your cloak, do not withhold even your tunic. [30] Give to everyone who asks of you, and from the one who takes what is yours do not demand it back. [31] Do to others as you would have them do to you. [32] For if you love those who love you, what credit is that to you? Even sinners love those who love them. [33] And if you do good to those who do good to you, what credit is that to you? Even sinners do the same. [34] If you lend money to those from

whom you expect repayment, what credit [is] that to you? Even sinners lend to sinners, and get back the same amount. [35] But rather, love your enemies and do good to them, and lend expecting nothing back; then your reward will be great and you will be children of the Most High, for he himself is kind to the ungrateful and the wicked. [36] Be merciful, just as your Father is merciful.

[37] "Stop judging and you will not be judged. Stop condemning and you will not be condemned. Forgive and you will be forgiven. [38] Give and gifts will be given to you; a good measure, packed together, shaken down, and overflowing, will be poured into your lap. For the measure with which you measure will in return be measured out to you."

Lectio

Jesus has a plan to draw men and women into his company. He uses healings to draw large crowds into his company. Once they gather he engages them as a preacher, stirring their hearts toward a deeper commitment to himself and the message. All this prepares for the opportunity to teach them about what life will be like as his students in the kingdom of God.

This week Jesus the preacher transitions to Jesus the teacher as he continues the Sermon on the Plain. Last week we saw the large crowds gather to hear Jesus preach. Now they are ready.

Jesus the master teacher begins by laying down his command that if they are to be his disciples they are going to have to love their enemies and do good to those who hate them. He expects his followers to bless those who curse them and pray for those who mistreat them. The biblical idea of love differs from the modern sense of the word. In the Bible you demonstrate love by remaining attached and in relationship with others, typically members of your family group. Conversely, when someone hates in the biblical world they have detached themselves from an interpersonal relationship. *Love* is to stay connected. *Hate* is to break connection. Recall the challenging teaching of Jesus from Luke 14:26 that to be his disciple we will have to love him and hate even our parents. On the surface this is absurd, but seen in this light it is an invitation to detach yourself from parental provision and attach yourself to Jesus as your teacher.

Jesus continues. If a person strikes you on the cheek, offer him the other. Don't retaliate; allow time for another person to intervene. Keep the peace. If someone wants to take your cloak do not refuse your tunic (an inner garment). If anyone takes what is yours, do not demand it back. These are the high expectations Jesus sets for those who want to follow him.

Where would potential disciples find themselves in these particular situations? Jesus is most likely referring to encounters with the Roman military, agents of those who rule Israel with an iron fist! Soldiers could strike you at any time. Don't fight back. They could demand your cloak. If they do, embarrass them by offering your tunic as well. If they take your donkey, don't waste your time demanding that it be returned. They can force you to go out of your way for a single mile, so offer to go two! Double down. Stay connected! Be a witness at all times.

Then Jesus teaches the "golden rule." Do to others as you would have them do to you. This is another high calling. Jesus reminds the disciples that even sinners love their friends and family—and to what credit? Why should you be honored if you only love those who already love you? Jesus wants his followers to love their enemies, even military overlords who embody oppression. They are to do good to enemies who hate them!

You live this way to be a witness. God sends his rain on the just and the unjust. Jesus promises that obedience to this teaching will result in a great reward in heaven. In addition, his disciples will also be called children of the Most High—children of God. They will be God's agents in the world, revealing to saint and sinner that the Most High is kind even to the ungrateful and the wicked. Jesus demands that his disciples not judge, not condemn, and not withhold forgiveness—from family members or from enemies. This is a real challenge! Jesus gives it to men and women who have experienced him as healer and preacher. Now they know him as teacher, as one whose instruction carries a unique authority. What will their response be? What is yours?

═══════════════ *Meditatio* ═══════════════

Stop judging. Stop condemning. Then you will not be judged or condemned yourself. Forgive and you will be forgiven. This has been an ongoing challenge for Christians. The author of John's Gospel felt a need to remind his community that "God did not send his Son into the world to condemn the world, but [sent him so] that the world might be saved through him" (John 3:17). It seems that even the early church needed continual reminders that Jesus came into the world to save sinners. That was his calling, and it becomes ours as well. It is easy to fall into a habit of judgment and condemnation. When we judge and condemn we shut out the Holy Spirit and deprive the Spirit of an opportunity to break through old barriers and shine a new light in the world. In Christ our one-time enemies can become our new brothers, sisters, friends.

You and I don't, by and large, live in a world with enemies so obvious as the Romans in the time of Jesus. They ruled with a brutal efficiency that crushed any who dared to oppose their empire. It is against that backdrop that Jesus challenges his disciples to love. He challenges his disciples to find ways to attach themselves to lifelong enemies so that even *those* enemies can be transformed by the message of salvation. What does that look like for you? Who do you consider an enemy? Can you see past the pain and separation into the soul of that person? Try to see them as God sees them, remembering that he is kind and merciful. God sends the rain on both just and unjust. Think about this as you prepare for church this week.

Oratio

Our prayer response this week will be the Peace Prayer of St. Francis. *Lord, make me an instrument of your peace: where there is hatred, let me sow love; where there is injury, pardon; where there is doubt, faith; where there is despair, hope; where there is darkness, light; where there is sadness, joy.*

O divine Master, grant that I may not so much seek to be consoled as to console, to be understood as to understand, to be loved as to love. For it is in giving that we receive, it is in pardoning that we are pardoned, and it is in dying that we are born to eternal life.

Contemplatio

We learn from our Jewish brothers and sisters in faith that deeds surpass creeds in the eyes of our loving God. Don't tell me what you believe, show me by your actions, by the way you live your life of faith for the world to see. The New Testament author of the letter of James reveals the same principle. He promises to "demonstrate [his] faith to you [by his] works" (James 2:14–18). You will recognize authentic Christians by the way they act around others. So what is the Jesus challenge this week? The Gospel ends with an admonition to give to others knowing that when you do so, God will be inclined to give gifts generously to you!

Where to begin? The threefold obligations of a Jewish person of faith are to pray (twice daily), fast (one day a year), and give alms (generously and consistently to all who are almsworthy). Try to put your faith in action this week. Pray that Jesus will show you people in need. When they are revealed to you, give generously. This active expression of faith will please the Father and will be a blessing for you too.

OTHER READINGS: 1 SAMUEL 26:2, 7–9, 12–13, 22–23; 1 CORINTHIANS 15:45–49

EIGHTH SUNDAY IN ORDINARY TIME

KNOWN BY ITS FRUIT

LUKE 6:39-45

³⁹ And he told them a parable, "Can a blind person guide a blind person? Will not both fall into a pit? ⁴⁰ No disciple is superior to the teacher; but when fully trained, every disciple will be like his teacher. ⁴¹ Why do you notice the splinter in your brother's eye, but do not perceive the wooden beam in your own? ⁴² How can you say to your brother, 'Brother, let me remove that splinter in your eye,' when you do not even notice the wooden beam in your own eye? You hypocrite! Remove the wooden beam from your eye first; then you will see clearly to remove the splinter in your brother's eye.

⁴³ "A good tree does not bear rotten fruit, nor does a rotten tree bear good fruit. ⁴⁴ For every tree is known by its own fruit. For people do not pick figs from thornbushes, nor do they gather grapes from brambles. ⁴⁵ A good person out of the store of goodness in his heart produces

good, but an evil person out of a store of evil produces evil; for from the fullness of the heart the mouth speaks."

Lectio

This week we return to Jesus's Sermon on the Plain. Here Jesus begins to speak in parables, creative stories or images designed to shock the audience. The shock element arrests the listener and leaves the mind in doubt as to the parable's precise meaning. The parable's challenge drives its message home. No one had ever taught like this before or would again. Teaching in parables—created on the spot—is a style unique to Jesus and reveals his genius.

The images in this week's parables are almost vaudevillian. Jesus must have spent time around actors and the stage. He calls some religious leaders hypocrites when he wants to shame them in public. The word *hypocrite* (in Greek) loosely defines the role of an actor: someone who presents themselves to others as another person while performing. The image of a pair of "blind guides" trying to lead one another, or anyone else for that matter, is quite comical. You could pull this scene off easily (and without much risk of bodily harm) on a local stage.

Another vaudevillian image is suggested in the parable about the beam and the splinter. Envisage the characters on stage: A person nearly blinded by a two by four in his eye struts around, comically confident that he can remove a small splinter of wood from the eye of his brother.

Jesus uses these two parabolic images to show how foolish both would be in real life. The blind cannot lead the blind. Someone with a beam in their eye will not be able see well enough to extract a splinter from the eye of anyone else, no matter how they try.

Where did Jesus acquire this knowledge about stagecraft? He grew up in the rural ridgetop village of Nazareth. Did he attend a theatre there? No. But there was a Roman theatre in the resort city of Sepphoris, jewel of the Galilee. This opulent Roman enclave was built during his lifetime. This large construction project may have been a source of work for a young Jesus and his adoptive father Joseph. One can easily imagine Jesus, on a break from construction work, watching masked actors rehearse on the

Sepphoris stage, pretending to be persons other than themselves. Could this experience have birthed his awareness of the hypocrites, the religious actors on the stage of life, who are blind themselves but still feel they can direct the lives of others? What we do know is that in the earliest centuries of the church the profession of acting (along with being an innkeeper or a prostitute!) was forbidden for Christians.

The use of parables in the Gospel of Luke will reveal Jesus's unique ability to engage and hold the attention of an audience he intends to teach and transform. The parables worked for him then, and properly understood will work in us now.

--- *Meditatio* ---

Jesus wants his disciples to know that a tree is known by its fruit. The fig tree cannot not produce dates. The date palm cannot produce figs. What spiritual fruit is most evident in your life? Use the list of the fruit of the Holy Spirit in Galatians 5:22–23 for this meditative exercise. The listed fruits of a life lived in the Spirit are love, joy, peace, patience, kindness, goodness, faithfulness, gentleness, and self-control. These are enough to get you started. Which of these is most evident in your life? How is it revealed to others? What would a friend say is the best fruit that your life reveals on a daily basis? As you conclude your inventory take a few moments to identify the fruit that reveals the best "you" to the world as you ask the Lord for the grace to grow more of that fruit so that it will be even more obvious to those whom you see and serve this week.

--- *Oratio* ---

In John 15 Jesus reveals to the disciples that he is the vine and they are the branches. If they stay connected to him they will bear abundant fruit. Apart from him they will wither and die. Lean into John 15:7–9 in prayer this week. *"If you remain in me and my words remain in you, ask for whatever you want and it will be done for you. By this is my Father glorified, that you bear much fruit and become my disciples. As the Father has loved me, so I also love you. Remain in my love."*

Words matter. Jesus teaches that it is out of the abundance of the heart that the mouth speaks. In the New Testament the heart is the seat of emotively infused thought. You think with your heart in the Middle Eastern world into which the Lord was born; the brain and the heart work in tandem. Thinking with your heart translates to thinking with your mind in the Western world. The words we speak and the way we speak them reveal what is going on in our mind. Words spoken cannot be taken back. Words can be used to bless or curse. Jesus wants us to know that our words and our manner reveal our inner character.

Once I was identified as a Christian on a golf course simply because, when I missed a short putt I exclaimed "Oh shoot!" rather than some other turn of phrase. As it turns out, the woman who identified me as a Christian by my choice of "words" asked me to pray for her. She was undergoing therapy for stage-four cancer. I promised I would and have ever since. A year later I met her again on the same course and reminded her of my commitment to pray for her. I was delighted to see her doing so well. She is on the mend, praise God! I am grateful that out of the abundance of my heart my mouth spoke words appropriate for a Christian on a golf course that day. God does work in mysterious and wonderful ways.

OTHER READINGS: SIRACH 27:5–8; 1 CORINTHIANS 15:54–58

FIRST SUNDAY IN LENT

RESIST THE DEVIL

LUKE 4:1-13

[1] Filled with the holy Spirit, Jesus returned from the Jordan and was led by the Spirit into the desert [2] for forty days, to be tempted by the devil. He ate nothing during those days, and when they were over he was hungry. [3] The devil said to him, "If you are the Son of God, command this stone to become bread." [4] Jesus answered him, "It is written, 'One

does not live by bread alone.'" [5] Then he took him up and showed him all the kingdoms of the world in a single instant. [6] The devil said to him, "I shall give to you all this power and their glory; for it has been handed over to me, and I may give it to whomever I wish. [7] All this will be yours, if you worship me." [8] Jesus said to him in reply, "It is written:

'You shall worship the Lord, your God,
and him alone shall you serve.'"

[9] Then he led him to Jerusalem, made him stand on the parapet of the temple, and said to him, "If you are the Son of God, throw yourself down from here, [10] for it is written:

'He will command his angels concerning you, to guard you,'

[11] and:

'With their hands they will support you,
lest you dash your foot against a stone.'"

[12] Jesus said to him in reply, "It also says, 'You shall not put the Lord, your God, to the test.'" [13] When the devil had finished every temptation, he departed from him for a time.

—————————— *Lectio* ——————————

The reading this week is Luke's account of the three temptations Jesus faces in the Judean wilderness immediately after his baptism. Our Gospel author is a Gentile convert to the faith, which may explain why he records the order of the temptations differently than Matthew, a Jewish believer. In Matthew's account, Jesus returns from the wilderness and sums up his experience by recounting to his disciples three specific temptations that he faced, in an order that demonstrates that Jesus is a true Israelite. Luke arranges the last two temptations to focus on Jesus in Jerusalem.

This scene opens after the baptism of Jesus when the voice of God echoes from the heavens: "You are my beloved Son; with you I am well pleased" (Luke 3:22). This is a claim of honor made by God about his Son, and the first century reader will not be surprised that Jesus is immediately led into the desert for testing. In the honor-and-shame culture of the Middle East, any public claim to honor evokes a public challenge.

To understand the temptation narrative we have to recall the daily prayer of the Jewish person of faith, the "Shema" from Deuteronomy 6:4–5 where the faithful pray to able to love the Lord God with their whole heart, soul, and strength. In the Middle East, the heart corresponds to our Western notion of the mind. The soul implies a body animated so that it can produce good works. Strength refers to what our mind and body produce when aligned with the purposes of God—our fruitfulness, to be shared with those in need. To live in such alignment, such balance, will reveal Jesus as a true Israelite—and thus as a candidate for Messiah.

Jesus bests the devil in temptations targeted at heart, soul, and strength. First, the devil wants Jesus to change his mind (his heart) about his mission. Don't bother with the messianic vision. Just end world hunger by turning stones into bread. But Jesus responds out of Deuteronomy to make his point: man does not live on bread alone but rather on every word that comes from the mouth of God!

Luke records the devil's second temptation as an offer to receive all the world's wealth and power—and it was his to give—if Jesus will just bow down to him. Here Jesus reminds the devil that Scripture teaches that you shall worship the Lord and serve him alone.

The third temptation has the devil trying to entice Jesus to throw his body from the highest point of the temple, trusting that God will save him from harm. Jesus gets the better of the devil again, quoting the Scripture that you do not put God to the test. The devil is defeated. Jesus is the victor. Now he and his growing band of disciples are free to make their way to Galilee. With the disciples confident that Jesus has overcome the enemy, he can begin his public ministry.

————————————— *Meditatio* —————————————

There is a unique power in the Word of God revealed by Jesus in these exchanges with the devil. Three times the devil tries to tempt Jesus to sin and three times Jesus responds with a passage from Scripture that sets the tempter back on his heels. "One does not live on bread alone." "You shall worship the Lord your God, and him alone shall you serve." "You shall not put the Lord your God to the test."

Hebrews 4:12 instructs us that "the word of God is living and active, sharper than any two-edged sword, penetrating even between soul and spirit, joints and marrow, and able to discern reflections and thought of the heart." There is power in the Word of God. There is authority in the Word of God. We meet our God in the Word. We need to know the Word and have the ability to rest on its promises and lean into it as a defense against temptation. Chose a new verse (or verses) to memorize and meditate on this week.

Oratio

O God, come to my assistance. O Lord, make haste to help me. Do not subject me to the final test but deliver me from the evil one. Amen.

Contemplatio

In the letter from James, the bishop of the Jerusalem church and brother of Jesus tells the church to submit ourselves to God and to resist the devil (James 4:7). We have all been tempted. We will all be tempted. We need a strategy that will keep us safe from the wiles of the enemy. Jesus is able to resist the devil in the wilderness by quoting passages from the Bible. Even when the devil attempts to mislead him by quoting from the Bible himself (in this case a passage from Psalm 91), Jesus is able to counter the devil's false interpretation.

Bishop James offers sound and practical advice. Submit to God—know that God is willing and able to deliver you from evil. Then, resist the devil "and he will flee from you." Each week we submit ourselves to God when we gather with other believers to worship, praise, and receive from the Lord. We are strengthened to resist the devil and his tempting schemes when we stay close to God in the Word, allowing the Word to be the lamp that guides our feet and the light that illuminates our path (Psalm 119:105). Draw near to God, James says, and God will draw near to you (James 2:8). That will be our action response this week.

OTHER READINGS: DEUTERONOMY 26:4–10; ROMANS 10:8–13

UP THE MOUNTAIN

LUKE 9:28b-36

²⁸ He took Peter, John, and James and went up the mountain to pray. ²⁹ While he was praying his face changed in appearance and his clothing became dazzling white. ³⁰ And behold, two men were conversing with him, Moses and Elijah, ³¹ who appeared in glory and spoke of his exodus that he was going to accomplish in Jerusalem. ³² Peter and his companions had been overcome by sleep, but becoming fully awake, they saw his glory and the two men standing with him. ³³ As they were about to part from him, Peter said to Jesus, "Master, it is good that we are here; let us make three tents, one for you, one for Moses, and one for Elijah." But he did not know what he was saying. ³⁴ While he was still speaking, a cloud came and cast a shadow over them, and they became frightened when they entered the cloud. ³⁵ Then from the cloud came a voice that said, "This is my chosen Son; listen to him." ³⁶ After the voice had spoken, Jesus was found alone. They fell silent and did not at that time tell anyone what they had seen.

Lectio

The Gospel opens eight days after Jesus gives the first of three passion predictions warning his disciples that he is going to Jerusalem where he will suffer "greatly and be rejected by the elders … and be killed and on the third day be raised" (Luke 9:22). He challenges his listeners to take up their cross and follow him to Jerusalem, before promising that some of those listening to his teaching would not taste death until they saw the kingdom of God. Here Jesus is not teaching about the final judgment but rather about a journey that he would invite Peter, James, and his brother John to take with him further into the mountains where he will be transfigured (imagine the instantaneous transformation of caterpillar to monarch butterfly!) before their eyes. These three apostles witness Jesus clothed in divine glory. This is their promised kingdom of God moment.

Jesus leaves Caesarea Philippi with Peter, James, and John and makes his way north toward the towering height of Mt. Hermon still in the distance. At an unknown location along the way Jesus pauses to pray. His disciples are wearied by the journey and fall asleep. Stirred from their slumber, they each see Jesus "transfigured," dressed in dazzling white garments. In addition, they see that he is speaking to the prophets Moses and Elijah. Luke tells us that the conversation had to do with the way Jesus would leave Jerusalem. Peter responds to what he sees in a most Jewish manner, and then a cloud covers the scene—the presence of God. The words are clearly heard by Peter and the others. Jesus has been revealed to them as a divine figure and the true Messiah of God.

Why Elijah? Why Moses? What do they have to teach us in the Transfiguration account? Moses is the narrative author of the Torah, the first five books of the Hebrew Bible. Elijah is the best representative of the Prophets, those who spoke to others in the name of the Lord. Elijah was unique. He did not die but was assumed into heaven, riding a fiery chariot that God sent to collect this great prophet. Moses had passed from this world to the next on the heights of Mt. Nebo (see Deuteronomy 34) but no one ever found his body or evidence of a grave. By the time of Jesus a traditional teaching had developed in Judaism that Moses, like Elijah, may have been assumed into heaven as well. Here, at the scene of the Transfiguration, Moses and Elijah appear and are speaking with Jesus about how he will depart from Jerusalem—about his assumption into heaven. It is worth noting that the story of the Ascension is found only in the Gospel of Luke. The message of Moses and Elijah is that Messiah has come and will please the Father when he lays down his life in Jerusalem.

This, then, explains Peter's unusual response that they busy themselves building tents (booths) to commemorate the event. This is the proper Jewish response to what they have witnessed. Seeing Jesus revealed in his divine glory is an assurance that the Messianic age of perfect provision is about to begin. Peter wants to begin what the prophet Zechariah said will be done when Jerusalem is restored. Everyone is to come to Jerusalem and celebrate the feast of Booths! (Zechariah 14:16) Peter is convinced. Jesus is the promised Messiah and the Son of God. It is time to get started building the booths to celebrate the festival. He does not understand that Jesus has more work to do. A cloud of glory covers the scene and the voice of God honors his Son: "Listen to him." It remains good advice today.

<hr>

Meditatio

Mountaintop moments. These are typically experiences of grace and blessing recalled from our past. We would like to see them continue long after we come back down and re-enter the workaday world. Peter, James, and John learn something about Jesus that the other apostles have yet to witness. Jesus swears them to secrecy (Matthew 17:9) until after he is raised from the dead. Unfortunately, this special knowledge will go straight to their heads. On the way back to Capernaum Jesus notices them arguing among themselves about who the greatest might be (Luke 9:46). Each of the three is convinced that they are the more favored by Jesus. Their experience on the mountain became a source of spiritual pride, a pride that Jesus will not allow. Jesus teaches the apostles that the one who wants to be the greatest among them needs to seek to be the least of all and the servant of the others.

What are your mountaintop memories? A pilgrimage? A retreat? A wilderness excursion? A church event that changed the course of your life of faith? These highs are hard to maintain but still valuable. They keep us hungry for more, filled with expectation that the ordinary can become the extraordinary once more. When it happens again don't let it go to your head. Receive the experience with a grateful heart and return from the mountain ready and willing to serve the least among us.

<hr>

Oratio

"This is my chosen Son; listen to him." Lord, open my ears because I want to hear Jesus. Send me your Spirit to inspire the desire to search for you in the Word so that I can hear you in the Word.

<hr>

Contemplatio

Our action response this week begins by looking at 2 Peter 1:16–18. Read this passage and see how the apostle Peter incorporates the "mountain-top" experience of the Transfiguration into his preaching. He remembers this experience as a source of hope as he senses that his time on this side of eternity may end soon. Jesus told Peter, James, and John not to speak about the Transfiguration until after he had conquered death by rising from the grave. Soon after the resurrection they certainly speak freely about their life-changing experience in the shadow of Mt. Hermon.

Recall moments of transformation in your spiritual journey. Times when you recall being in the Lord's presence. Look for an opportunity to share one of them this week. Share with someone how God used an unexpected event in your life to call you into a deeper relationship with Jesus.

OTHER READINGS: GENESIS 15:5–12, 17–18; PHILIPPIANS 3:17–4:1

THIRD SUNDAY OF LENT

IN SEARCH OF FRUIT

LUKE 13:1–9

[1] At that time some people who were present there told him about the Galileans whose blood Pilate had mingled with the blood of their sacrifices. [2] He said to them in reply, "Do you think that because these Galileans suffered in this way they were greater sinners than all other Galileans? [3] By no means! But I tell you, if you do not repent, you will all perish as they did! [4] Or those eighteen people who were killed when the tower at Siloam fell on them—do you think they were more guilty than everyone else who lived in Jerusalem? [5] By no means! But I tell you, if you do not repent, you will all perish as they did!"

[6] And he told them this parable: "There once was a person who had a fig tree planted in his orchard, and when he came in search of fruit on it but found none, [7] he said to the gardener, 'For three years now I have come in search of fruit on this fig tree but have found none. [So] cut it down. Why should it exhaust the soil?' [8] He said to him in reply, 'Sir, leave it for this year also, and I shall cultivate the ground around it and fertilize it; [9] it may bear fruit in the future. If not you can cut it down.'"

Politics and religion have never mixed well. In our Gospel portion this week, Jesus hears a report that Pilate, the representative of the Roman military authority in the province of Syria, is accused of executing Jews of Galilee so that their own blood is mixed with their sacrificial offerings. There is no record of this event outside of the Gospel but this sort of atrocity (exaggerated or not) fits the character of Pilate. According to the historian Josephus, Pilate was also responsible for the murder of innocent Samaritans worshiping on Mt. Gerizim. In another bloody incident he ordered the murder of several political opponents who challenged his right to rob the temple treasury to fund an aqueduct project that would bring more water to the temple area. In each instance Pilate's orders lead to the death of innocent men. It seems he is at it again.

Those who bring Jesus the report emphasize that the dead are Galileans. They hope to incite a politically charged response. As a Galilean himself, Jesus should be loyal to their cause and harbor ill will toward the Roman overlords. After all, Jesus has recently taught that he has been sent to "set the earth on fire," wishing that "it were already blazing" (Luke 12:49). In that same teaching Jesus says that he has not been sent to bring peace on the earth but rather division (Luke 12:51). Perhaps these recent statements encouraged those who report to Jesus what Pilate has done in Jerusalem.

This is a public challenge. Jesus knows that those making the report are trying to trip him up. Is he a true Galilean? Will he support their cause? Or is he a Roman collaborator? Much hangs in the balance before Jesus responds with a question of his own and wins the exchange. Jesus reminds the messengers that the Galileans who died were no greater sinners than any others—and adds that they are all going to go to the grave eventually. Repent in the time you have left! Turn around and come back to God!

Jesus reminds them that a large tower had recently collapsed and killed eighteen people by the Pool of Siloam. What caused the tragedy? Probably an earthquake. Israel is situated in a highly seismic area. Those who died when the tower fell were simply in the wrong place and time. Jesus again reminds the messengers that if they are alive to hear this report there is still time to repent and come back to the Father.

Jesus uses the parable of the barren fig tree to summarize his teaching. According to Levitical law you are required to wait four years before you consume any fruit of a new tree (Leviticus 19:23–25). In the parable, the landowner has looked for evidence of fruit for three years and finds none. The tree is barren and should be cut down and replaced by another, fruitful tree. Its time is up; judgment must follow. The gardener in the parable, a biblical image of God himself (Isaiah 5:1–7), has a better idea. He suggests more care, more hope. He asks for more time, just one more year. If the tree does not bear fruit (repent?) then it can be cut down. Jesus uses this parable to connect the deadly wrath of Pilate and the accident at Siloam to his story. The time was up for those who died. Those still alive to hear the parable have time to repent, to return to God and begin to produce fruit so that they can live. A message of the parable is that even the giver of the law is merciful, providing every opportunity for the tree to produce fruit and remain in the orchard.

Meditatio

The parables of Jesus are unique stories created on the spur of the moment. Jesus draws his inspiration from nature or common life and tells an open-ended story that always has a shock element and leaves the listener in some doubt as to his precise meaning. Jesus only teaches in parables when large crowds gather around him and when he will not have time for individual explanation. You and I, like those in the original audience, are required to work out the spiritual math for ourselves. The parable teachings of Jesus reveal his genius to the world.

Our meditation this week reminds us that there is still time. Time to live. Time to breathe. And time to repent. The message of the parable is that ultimately our time is limited. The fig tree had not produced fruit for three years. It was time for it to be cut down. Only the surprise appearance of a merciful gardener saves the tree, granting it one more year to blossom and produce fruit. We are living in that spiritual year now, a time of grace that affords us an opportunity to assess our spiritual life and the fruit that it is producing. We too can repent and return to the God who loves us and is always calling us back.

Lent is a season for spiritual self-reflection. What would the Gardener of your soul suggest to help you produce more fruit in your life? Do you need more nutrients (the Word)? More water (the Spirit)? More manure? Imagine what that gardener would prescribe for you and in your meditation see the plan through to completion.

———————————————— *Oratio* ————————————————

Death will call for us all. As Christians our hope is in the Lord and in his victory over the grave. We are all going home. Paul states emphatically that "Death is swallowed up in victory" and wonders, "Where, O death, is your victory? Where, O death is your sting?" (1 Corinthians 15:54–55).

Thank you, Jesus for conquering the grave and for the promise of the final defeat of death. I pray that my soul will find rest when it finally rests in you. Amen.

———————————————— *Contemplatio* ————————————————

As an action response this week, take a few moments to reflect on those who have "gone before us, marked with the sign of faith" and are now with the Lord. The church teaches that love conquers death and the grave. The faithful who have died with Christ are now alive with the Lord and in communion with those of us on this side of eternity. They have gone home, and we are on the way.

Can you recall the circumstances of their passing? Was it peaceful? Full of grace? Do you recall the emotions you felt at their passing? Who did you know that died well? What about that passing spoke to you? How was God present in that moment? These are suitable considerations in this season of Lent. Take time this week to consider these questions and pray for a good death when your time comes, a death that will remind those around you of your hope and trust in the Lord.

OTHER READINGS: EXODUS 3:1–8a, 13–15; 1 CORINTHIANS 10:1–6, 10–12

TWO SONS

LUKE 15:1-3, 11-32

[1] The tax collectors and sinners were all drawing near to listen to him, [2] but the Pharisees and scribes began to complain, saying, "This man welcomes sinners and eats with them." [3] So to them he addressed this parable.

[11] Then he said, "A man had two sons, [12] and the younger son said to his father, 'Father, give me the share of your estate that should come to me.' So the father divided the property between them. [13] After a few days, the younger son collected all his belongings and set off to a distant country where he squandered his inheritance on a life of dissipation. [14] When he had freely spent everything, a severe famine struck that country, and he found himself in dire need. [15] So he hired himself out to one of the local citizens who sent him to his farm to tend the swine. [16] And he longed to eat his fill of the pods on which the swine fed, but nobody gave him any. [17] Coming to his senses he thought, 'How many of my father's hired workers have more than enough food to eat, but here am I, dying from hunger. [18] I shall get up and go to my father and I shall say to him, "Father, I have sinned against heaven and against you. [19] I no longer deserve to be called your son; treat me as you would treat one of your hired workers."' [20] So he got up and went back to his father. While he was still a long way off, his father caught sight of him, and was filled with compassion. He ran to his son, embraced him and kissed him. [21] His son said to him, 'Father, I have sinned against heaven and against you; I no longer deserve to be called your son.' [22] But his father ordered his servants, 'Quickly bring the finest robe and put it on him; put a ring on his finger and sandals on his feet. [23] Take the fattened calf and slaughter it. Then let us celebrate with a feast, [24] because this son of mine was dead, and has come to life again; he was lost, and has been found.' Then the celebration began. [25] Now the older son had been out in the field and, on his way back, as he neared the house, he heard the sound

of music and dancing. ²⁶ He called one of the servants and asked what this might mean. ²⁷ The servant said to him, 'Your brother has returned and your father has slaughtered the fattened calf because he has him back safe and sound.' ²⁸ He became angry, and when he refused to enter the house, his father came out and pleaded with him. ²⁹ He said to his father in reply, 'Look, all these years I served you and not once did I disobey your orders; yet you never gave me even a young goat to feast on with my friends. ³⁰ But when your son returns who swallowed up your property with prostitutes, for him you slaughter the fattened calf.' ³¹ He said to him, 'My son, you are here with me always; everything I have is yours. ³² But now we must celebrate and rejoice, because your brother was dead and has come to life again; he was lost and has been found.'"

Lectio

Jesus teaches in parables when he needs to address a large group. This unique style of creating an engaging story to make a theological point reveals his creative genius. Each parable is intended to shock the listening audience and leave them doubtful of its precise meaning and application.

This parable sends seismic shock waves to unsettle the religious leaders who have challenged Jesus. Two opposing groups gather. Tax collectors (Roman collaborators) and other public outcasts sit across from the scribes and Pharisees, the religious professionals. The religious leaders wonder how Jesus can eat with these sinners and not be defiled. It is to this audience that Jesus directs his most compelling parable to date.

The man with two sons is the main character in the parable and represents God. The older of his two sons appears compliant and obedient, the younger is restless and reckless. These are stock characters for storytellers in Jesus's day. The audience would have been shocked to hear the younger son ask for his share of the estate. What's more, he speaks to his father using the Greek imperative tense. This is a demand, and not a request! The next shock occurs when the father actually divides the estate. This is expressly prohibited in Jewish law (Sirach 33:20–24). The father knows this but still divides the estate between his sons, bringing shame upon himself in the process. He knows he is dead in the eyes of his younger son. His older son is likewise implicated by his callous disregard for his father's honor. As the eldest he would have been expected to intervene as an agent of reconciliation between the other two characters in the parable. The father has effectively lost both boys in one fell swoop!

Things get worse. The younger son takes his inheritance and travels to Gentile territory. In a few years' time he loses everything he has to live on. He is reduced to hiring himself out to tend a flock of ritually unclean swine. His faith hangs by a thread. As a swineherd he would be allowed to eat the meat of the animals he tends. He rejects this option and finds himself starving as a result. He needs a plan. His one hope is in returning to his father as a hired man. He is sure he will not be received back as a son.

The plot thickens. The younger son devises a plan to demand that his father hire him as a servant; he will at least have food to eat. When he does return he is shocked to see his father running toward him. Men of age and acquired honor do not run in the Middle East. This will not turn out well for the younger son. Then his father reaches him, embraces him, and receives him as an equal with a cheek-to-cheek kiss. His father clothes him in the best robe, gives him a signet ring to restore his status as his son, and makes sure he has shoes on his feet. He is not going to be a servant in his house but will be reinstated as a son. The father shocks the entire village by ordering the fattened calf slaughtered. That animal will feed over one hundred people! All will be invited to celebrate the return of this lost son.

We meet the older son returning home. We are shocked to learn of his unwillingness to go into the house to serve as his father's representative at the celebration. Finally his father has to shame himself again by leaving the house to beg his older son to come in. His younger brother was dead and has come back to life. He pleads with the older son: they must celebrate. The older brother accuses his younger sibling of living a life of dissipation that brings shame on the family (Proverbs 29:3). He may be a "son of yours" but he is no "brother of mine" and there the parable ends. Abruptly. What will the older brother do? Will he go with the father into the house and greet the guests who have gathered to celebrate, or remain outside in opposition? We just don't know. The parable challenges us to make up our own minds about the outcome.

The word *prodigal* is defined as "reckless" and "wasteful." This adjective fits the younger son. He was certainly reckless and wasteful of his share of the estate and of his relationship to his father. His father has to liquidate land from his ancestral estate to fund the departure of his prodigal son.

Perhaps more compelling is our consideration of the father in the parable, clearly meant to be an image of God in the way that he is willing to address each of his wayward sons. His older son is estranged from his father with the Law. His younger son is equally estranged; living a life without the Law of God in his heart. The prodigal father reaches out to both sons. Both are lost. Both need to find their way home. The prodigal father is "reckless" and "wasteful" in his all-consuming love for both. He risks shame and ridicule in his village and among his relatives when he agrees to the demands of his younger son. He faces public scorn again when he leaves the celebration to publicly beg that his other son return with him to the celebration of reunion.

The father comes full circle in regard to younger son. Once lost, we have begun the celebration of his return. What about his eldest? Will the father's pleas go unheeded? Will his older son respond to his invitation to return to the house? We don't know. That is the genius of the parable.

So, who are you in the parable? The restless and reckless younger son who already sees his father as dead in his eyes? The older and seemingly more orthodox brother biding his time until his father dies? What is it about the father and his responses to each son that speaks to you? What actions of the father reveal the love God has for us? Is it his willingness to be shamed? The patient watch he maintains until his son returns? His heartfelt desire to greet and kiss his lost son? His tender mercy toward his eldest son? There is much to consider in our meditation this week.

Oratio

Lord, open my heart so that I can realize and understand your deep and abiding love. Forgive me when I turn away from you. Wait for me while I gather the courage to return. Receive me with the grace of an embrace of love when I do.

The challenge this week is to find yourself in the parable. Which character do you identify with the most? Are you the older son? Have you always been with the father but have lost connection with his love? Are you a younger son? Anxious and restless? Could you see yourself demanding of your father your inheritance so that you can head out on your own?

When you prayerfully identify yourself as an actor in the parable be willing to receive the father's loving embrace and words of consolation. The father offers both to each of his sons. Each has strayed in their own way. Both need to find their way back home, and so do we. The father in the parable—God—can sometimes be reckless in his overwhelming love for his children. That is good news this week.

OTHER READINGS: JOSHUA 5:9a, 10–12; 2 CORINTHIANS 5:17–21

FIFTH SUNDAY OF LENT

FROM NOW ON

JOHN 8:1–11

[1] Jesus went to the Mount of Olives. [2] But early in the morning he arrived again in the temple area, and all the people started coming to him, and he sat down and taught them. [3] Then the scribes and the Pharisees brought a woman who had been caught in adultery and made her stand in the middle. [4] They said to him, "Teacher, this woman was caught in the very act of committing adultery. [5] Now in the law, Moses commanded us to stone such women. So what do you say?" [6] They said this to test him, so that they could have some charge to bring against him. Jesus bent down and began to write on the ground with his finger. [7] But when they continued asking him, he straightened up and said to them, "Let the one among you who is without sin be the first to throw a stone at her." [8] Again he bent down and wrote on the ground. [9] And in response, they went away one by one, beginning with the elders. So he

was left alone with the woman before him. ¹⁰ Then Jesus straightened up and said to her, "Woman, where are they? Has no one condemned you?" ¹¹ She replied, "No one, sir." Then Jesus said, "Neither do I condemn you. Go, [and] from now on do not sin any more."

—————————————— *Lectio* ——————————————

In the Gospel this week Jesus comes to the temple mount early in the morning. Immediately men gather to hear him teach (women will come to the area later in the morning). Jesus is recognized as an esteemed teacher and is accorded the honor of sitting in the midst of his disciples. As he is teaching, a raucous group of religious leaders push through the disciples standing around him. They force a terrified woman to stand in front of the group and claim that she was caught in the very act of adultery.

She stands shamed in the midst of these men as they challenge Jesus with a premeditated "theological" question. They remind Jesus that the law of Moses commands that such a woman be stoned to death (see Deuteronomy 22:22, and note how the man who was caught in the act with her is conveniently missing). What will the teacher have them do? They want his opinion. Will he side with Moses and the strict interpretation of the law, allowing them to stone her to death? If so, they can report him to the Roman officials who have forbidden Jews from carrying out capital punishment on their own. Or will Jesus deny the law and be branded a blasphemer? Their plan to shame Jesus seems to be working, until …

Jesus takes control of the scene. He bends down and doodles on the paving stones. Why is he doing this? What is he writing? All eyes are drawn to Jesus. It's a clever move. He draws their attention from her to himself. Jesus doesn't give her even a glance! People in our culture might see this as a sign of disrespect, but Jesus knows she has been shamed enough by these men and wants to ease her pain. It works. The men who have surely been ogling the woman are no longer paying any attention to her. She has an opportunity to collect herself and regain some modicum of honor by adjusting her clothes and covering her hair.

All eyes are fixed Jesus when he finally announces his shocking response to their challenge. Yes, they should stone her. Does Jesus really agree that this is the proper punishment for an offense against the marital bond? But if they are going to stone her, he says, the first person to cast a stone must be the one among them who has never sinned.

Execution by stoning was a communal affair. Everyone had to participate or the sentence would be commuted. Jesus knows that anyone who would cast a stone, and in so doing claim that they are without sin, would be shamed by the community. He bends down again. We learn that the older men are the first to drop their stones. The younger men follow suit.

Jesus is alone with the woman. He stands up. He may not even be looking at her when he speaks. We can imagine the gentle and consoling tone he uses as he calls her "woman," a term of endearment Jesus also uses in addressing his own mother Mary. As used here it translates as "my dear one." The unexpected note of affection would convey comfort to the woman exposed in her sin. "Where are they? Has no one condemned you?" Jesus asks these two questions without making eye contact, a way of honoring her and reinforcing the words to follow: He will not condemn her either. She is free to leave, having heard his direction to sin no more.

—————————————— *Meditatio* ——————————————

What did Jesus write on the ground that day? Have you ever wondered? I read once that Jesus bent down and began to list sins that a man might have committed in his life. Envy, slander, sloth, anger, rage, lust … Maybe Jesus used this opportunity to remind the crowd that everyone has sinned and that this woman is no different than themselves. They, like her, are also in need of God's mercy and forgiveness. Other scholars suggest that Jesus wrote down the men's personal names. Jesus knows they set the woman up so they could bring their accusation that morning. She is a pawn in their vicious game.

Maybe Jesus didn't write anything at all and his distracting gesture is only meant to save face for a woman in the presence of her accusers. This simple, direct, and effective action gives him time to come up with a plan to turn the tables on the accusers and liberate the woman from her shame. Consider how blessed we are to see the merciful genius of Jesus on display in the Gospel this week.

The Jesus prayer is ancient and is meant to be memorized and repeated. It is a way that a Christian can "pray always" and reminds us that we need to be constantly aware of our need for Jesus and his forgiveness of our sins. Commit this prayer to memory and recite it often:

"Lord Jesus Christ, son of the living God, have mercy on me, a sinner."

———————————— *Contemplatio* ————————————

"Go, and from now on do not sin anymore." The woman hears these last words from Jesus ending her early morning ordeal. The horror and trauma of the previous hours, complete with the possibility of being stoned to death has come to a blessed end. In all the time Jesus has engaged with her and her accusers he never made eye contact. He honors her in a time of shame and leaves her with these gentle words of counsel. They are words we need to hear today, especially in the season of Lent. These words of Jesus echo those that the Catholic Christian hears in the Sacrament of Reconciliation. After we acknowledge and confess our sins we trust that those sins are forgiven in the name of the Father and the Son and the Holy Spirit (1 John 1:8–9). Then we do well to remember Jesus's words to this woman. "Go, and from now on do not sin anymore." Take a few moments to pray for the grace you need to turn away from sin toward God this week.

OTHER READINGS: ISAIAH 43:16–21; PHILIPPIANS 3:8–14

PALM SUNDAY

THE STONES WILL CRY OUT

LUKE 19:28-40

> [28] After he had said this, he proceeded on his journey up to Jerusalem. [29] As he drew near to Bethphage and Bethany at the place called the Mount of Olives, he sent two of his disciples. [30] He said, "Go into the village opposite you, and as you enter it you will find a colt tethered on which no one has ever sat. Untie it and bring it here. [31] And if anyone

should ask you, 'Why are you untying it?' you will answer, 'The Master has need of it.'" [32] So those who had been sent went off and found everything just as he had told them. [33] And as they were untying the colt, its owners said to them, "Why are you untying this colt?" [34] They answered, "The Master has need of it." [35] So they brought it to Jesus, threw their cloaks over the colt, and helped Jesus to mount. [36] As he rode along, the people were spreading their cloaks on the road; [37] and now as he was approaching the slope of the Mount of Olives, the whole multitude of his disciples began to praise God aloud with joy for all the mighty deeds they had seen. [38] They proclaimed:

"Blessed is the king
who comes in the name of the Lord.
Peace in heaven
and glory in the highest."

[39] Some of the Pharisees in the crowd said to him, "Teacher, rebuke your disciples." [40] He said in reply, "I tell you, if they keep silent, the stones will cry out!"

Lectio

This week we anticipate the celebration of Palm Sunday. This is the one Sunday of the year when we read two Gospel passages in the liturgy. I will focus on the opening Gospel that features the triumphal entry of Jesus into Jerusalem. The other passage is the Passion narrative from St. Luke.

Jesus makes his way to the highest point on the Mount of Olives after securing for himself a colt to ride (Matthew identifies it as a female donkey, along with her year-old foal). He plans to ride this small animal down into Jerusalem and has arranged in advance to have her ready. Why? He knows that many in the still-growing crowds that follow him now have expectations about how he might reveal himself as a conquering king, a challenger to Herod and the Romans who now control Jerusalem. He wants to make sure he looks comical rather than regal as he makes his way down the mountainside. The crowds do their best to change this message. They cover the colt with their cloaks and line the road with more cloaks (a sort of red-carpet treatment) to present Jesus as a potential rival to Rome.

This is not lost on Jesus. He has known that eventually it will come to this. He had to be ready in advance with this plan. Luke is the only Gospel writer who does not mention that many in the crowd had secured palm branches in anticipation of this entry. Luke is a Gentile follower of Jesus and would not likely have been familiar with the political significance of palm branches. But the other Gospels tell us that many in the crowd have branches that they are waving passionately. And they didn't get them from the roadside, since palm trees do not grow on the Mount of Olives.

These branches seem to have been secured, secretly, as people traveled through the "City of Palms"— Jericho. Why would they carry them such a long way? In the time of Jesus, the palm branch (not just a single frond) had become a symbol of Jewish liberation from oppression. The Maccabee family who drove Greek occupiers out of Jerusalem in 164 BC used palms to cleanse and rededicate the temple. Jewish patriots in the crowd brandish the palm branches as a secret symbol, unintelligible to the Romans, that Jesus, the new King of the Jews, is coming to depose Herod and his Roman backers from the throne.

The enthusiastic words of praise are spoken in Aramaic or Hebrew so the Romans will not understand. They capture the revolutionary sentiment: Jesus is the king who is coming in the name of the true Lord, Yahweh, and not in the name of the false lord, Caesar. In other Gospel accounts they cry out "hosanna," a word that carries the heartfelt petition that God "save us" from our oppressors. The waving palms intensify the message: We are coming for you, Herod! We are coming for you, Pilate!

All of this is said and done with smiles on countless faces and is completely misunderstood by the Roman guards who line the path down the mountain. How dangerous can this Jesus be? He is riding a female donkey after all. He would be considered no threat to anyone, certainly not to Herod or to Rome.

This also explains why some Pharisees want Jesus to silence his disciples. If the Romans find out what they are saying there will be a stiff price to pay! They are afraid, but Jesus is not. He takes it all in. The scene is alive with energy. Jesus reminds them that if the disciples were silenced every stone will cry out.

I am captivated by who might be among the thousands who surround Jesus that morning on his humble ride into Jerusalem. Most certainly there are the twelve apostles. Has it occurred to Judas yet that he might betray the Lord? Have Peter, James, and John sorted out among themselves who was the favored of the Lord? All three have witnessed his transfiguration. I wonder if the chief tax collector in the region, Zacchaeus—the one whose life Jesus saved in Jericho—has followed him to Jerusalem. We know that once-blind Bartimaeus made his way with Jesus from Jericho to Bethany. Is he there that morning? And what about Lazarus, raised from the grave after four days? He and his sisters lived in Bethany where they had often hosted Jesus and his apostles. What an all-star cast. And in the middle of the crowd is Jesus. Jesus, seated humbly and almost comically astride a small donkey. Are his feet dragging as she clip-clops her way down the well-worn path from Olivet and into Jerusalem?

And then there are the stones. Those famous stones are everywhere to be seen. The western-facing slope of the Mount of Olives is a popular burial site. People hoped that at the resurrection the deceased will rise to face the temple in all its restored glory. The stones that Jesus says will cry out were probably gravestones, the markers of men and women who have died in faith and know how this story, his story, will have to end. Blessed is Jesus, the true king who comes in the name of the Lord. I invite you to sit for a moment or two with these musings this week.

━━━━━━━━━━━━━ *Oratio* ━━━━━━━━━━━━

We will find our prayer response to this reading in Psalm 24:7–10. These verses capture the excitement of that day and the procession of Jesus from the heights of the Mount of Olives into Jerusalem on Palm Sunday.

"Lift up your heads, O gates; be lifted, you ancient portals, that the king of glory may enter. Who is this king of glory? The Lord, strong and mighty, the Lord, mighty in war. Lift up your heads, O gates; rise up, you ancient portals, that the king of glory may enter. Who is the king of glory? The Lord of hosts, he is the king of glory."

Do we know of stones that would cry out if they could? I think cemetery gravestones do exactly that. The messages on these stones remind us of who has gone before and what was most important to them. The gravestones remind us of lost loved ones and rekindle memories of their lives in our minds. As a faith response this week, if you can, visit a cemetery and honor the dead by reading their headstones and remembering their lives. These are stones that would cry out if they could. They mark the graves of men and women who have gone before us marked with the sign of faith. They now know what life is like on the other side of the grave. What do their stones say to you as you pass by?

OTHER READINGS: ISAIAH 50:4–7; PHILIPPIANS 2:6–11; LUKE 22:14–23:56

THE RESURRECTION OF THE LORD

WHAT COULD IT MEAN?

JOHN 20:1–9

[1] On the first day of the week, Mary of Magdala came to the tomb early in the morning, while it was still dark, and saw the stone removed from the tomb. [2] So she ran and went to Simon Peter and to the other disciple whom Jesus loved, and told them, "They have taken the Lord from the tomb, and we don't know where they put him." [3] So Peter and the other disciple went out and came to the tomb. [4] They both ran, but the other disciple ran faster than Peter and arrived at the tomb first; [5] he bent down and saw the burial cloths there, but did not go in. [6] When Simon Peter arrived after him, he went into the tomb and saw the burial cloths there, [7] and the cloth that had covered his head, not with the burial cloths but rolled up in a separate place. [8] Then the other disciple also went in, the one who had arrived at the tomb first, and he saw and believed. [9] For they did not yet understand the scripture that he had to rise from the dead.

This week we prepare to celebrate the resurrection. Jesus conquers the grave! The Gospel opens on Sunday, the first day of the week for the Jewish faith community. Very early in the morning, before even the first light of dawn, Mary of Magdala and other women arrive at the tomb and discover that it has been opened. The large stone has been moved aside and the burial chamber is empty. The body of Jesus is nowhere to be found!

Why are these women here? Apparently they intended to anoint the body of Jesus with additional aromatic spices to prepare his corpse for transport from the temporary tomb of Joseph of Arimathea to its final resting place, perhaps in Nazareth. Their plans are dashed when they find the tomb empty. Mary immediately runs into Jerusalem and finds Peter and "the other disciple," usually identified as John. She tells them she has been to the tomb. It is open, the stone has been rolled away, and it is empty. She does not have any idea where to look for the body of Jesus.

Events escalate quickly. Peter and John run to the tomb. John, younger and apparently swifter, outpaces Peter. He arrives at the entrance but only to peer inside. The body is missing but the cloths are left behind in an orderly manner. What could it mean? Would graverobbers take time to unwrap the body? Now Peter arrives. He enters and examines the scene more closely. He notes that the cloth used to cover the body of Jesus as a shroud and the linen strips used to cover his head lie in separate locations. These burial linens seem to be intact—later the church would speculate it was as if the body of Jesus simply rose through them. Peter considers what this might suggest. Finally John enters and after his careful examination of the evidence is convinced that Jesus must have risen from the dead, just as he had promised. John sees and believes.

This progression from doubt to faith is wonderfully revealed in the Greek text. In our English translations John and Peter come on the scene and simply look into the tomb. The Gospel reports what each one "saw." The Greek text reveals a deeper meaning. When John arrives at the tomb he sees in a manner that we typically use to translate the word "saw." In Greek he *blepo* or "saw," without any deeper understanding. Peter enters the tomb. What he "saw" translates the Greek *theoreo*: Peter sees and forms a theory about what it means. When John enters, what he "saw" translates the Greek word *eiden:* he came to an intelligent conclusion. John simply sees the empty tomb. Peter forms a theory based on what he sees, and then John enters and forms his final opinion. He sees and he believes. The tomb is empty because Jesus has risen from the dead!

Meditatio

Christians profess that Jesus has risen bodily from the grave. He then appeared to men and women for the next forty days, providing even more evidence of the resurrection. This belief can bear the weight of our most careful and rigorous examination, as we can see in John's account of the resurrection story. John reminds his readers that three well-known people—a woman and two men in his company of apostles—find the tomb empty and the body of Jesus missing. Each notes that the tomb is empty. The evidence of what has been left behind rules out the possibility that the grave has been robbed. His burial linens remain behind and intact while the body cannot be found. Each person who comes to the tomb has to work out the details for themselves. First Mary of Magdala, then the apostles Peter and John. Each comes to the conclusion that Jesus must have risen from the grave. Carefully examined, the evidence leads nowhere else.

Where are you in that process of critical examination? Which New Testament character speaks to your faith? Have you been as skeptical as Mary of Magdala, who came to the tomb expecting to find the body of Jesus and prepare it for safe passage to a final resting place? Can you relate more easily with Peter and John who were probably hiding behind locked doors in the upper room waiting for daylight to begin their journey back to Galilee? Recall that at least two other disciples follow this course and are met by Jesus on their way to their home village of Emmaus (see Luke 24). These two disciples meet the risen Jesus and share a meal with him. Or perhaps your meditation draws you to Peter and John in the empty tomb. John arrives first but is afraid to go in. Peter comes on the scene and enters the tomb. It takes time to comprehend that Jesus has risen just as he had promised. Now John enters the tomb; he sees and he believes. Who are you most like on that Easter morning?

This Easter exchange between believers is heard all over the world on Easter Sunday. "The Lord is risen!" We respond: "He is risen indeed!"

Reserve some time this week to read and compare the four Gospel accounts of the resurrection. Where are they similar (the tomb is empty in each account!) and where do they differ? What do the differences suggest? If all four accounts agreed in every detail might we imagine collusion among the authors? But our four authors (and St. Paul in 1 Corinthians 15) offer four slightly different accounts of the same event. What they hold in common are the keys that reveal the central truths of that Easter morning.

First, that women came to the tomb. Second, that the stone was rolled away from the entrance and the Roman guard had fled the scene. Third, the body of Jesus was missing but his burial clothes remained behind, not unwound but intact. These facts—and their later encounters with the risen Lord—convinced them that Jesus had risen from the grave, just as he had promised. The world as they knew it changed that day. What details about the resurrection story resonate with you?

OTHER READINGS: ACTS 10:34a, 37–43; COLOSSIANS 3:1–4

SECOND SUNDAY OF EASTER

MY LORD AND MY GOD

JOHN 20:19-31

¹⁹ On the evening of that first day of the week, when the doors were locked, where the disciples were, for fear of the Jews, Jesus came and stood in their midst and said to them, "Peace be with you." ²⁰ When he had said this, he showed them his hands and his side. The disciples rejoiced when they saw the Lord. ²¹ [Jesus] said to them again, "Peace be with you. As the Father has sent me, so I send you." ²² And when he had said this, he breathed on them and said to them, "Receive the

holy Spirit. ²³ Whose sins you forgive are forgiven them, and whose sins you retain are retained."

²⁴ Thomas, called Didymus, one of the Twelve, was not with them when Jesus came. ²⁵ So the other disciples said to him, "We have seen the Lord." But he said to them, "Unless I see the mark of the nails in his hands and put my finger into the nailmarks and put my hand into his side, I will not believe." ²⁶ Now a week later his disciples were again inside and Thomas was with them. Jesus came, although the doors were locked, and stood in their midst and said, "Peace be with you." ²⁷ Then he said to Thomas, "Put your finger here and see my hands, and bring your hand and put it into my side, and do not be unbelieving, but believe." ²⁸ Thomas answered and said to him, "My Lord and my God!" ²⁹ Jesus said to him, "Have you come to believe because you have seen me? Blessed are those who have not seen and have believed."

³⁰ Now Jesus did many other signs in the presence of [his] disciples that are not written in this book. ³¹ But these are written that you may [come to] believe that Jesus is the Messiah, the Son of God, and that through this belief you may have life in his name.

Lectio

I have my doubts about "Doubting Thomas." Do you? When we look at the apostle from the full perspective of the Gospel of John the unique character of the man Thomas is revealed. He is a man of faith and action. It seems a pity to have cast him as a doubter throughout Christian history.

The first time we meet Thomas in John is in chapter 11. Jesus has just learned that his good friend Lazarus is ill. Jesus and the apostles had left Judea in haste because religious leaders in Jerusalem are plotting to have him arrested and killed. The disciples know that a return to Bethany will imperil them all, but Thomas convinces the others to accompany Jesus. He is quoted in the Gospel as saying, "Let us also go to die with him." Inspired by his courage, they all return. If Thomas were a doubter by nature, it seems unlikely he would volunteer to head back into harm's way.

I wonder too why he is called Didymus. This name translates as "the twin." Is it possible that Thomas closely resembled another man in the apostolic group? Consider that Judas has to ensure that the guard arrests the correct person in the garden by identifying Jesus with a kiss. Did Thomas bear a strong physical resemblance to the Lord—maybe similar enough to be called his twin? We may never know, but it may explain why Judas is so concerned that Jesus alone is arrested that night.

On the evening of the resurrection Jesus appears to disciples gathered together, hiding behind locked doors in justified fear of reprisal from the authorities who had conspired to have Jesus executed. We don't know where this appearance takes place, though most scholars place the believers in the same upper room where they had recently celebrated Passover.

Jesus suddenly passes through those locked doors and speaks peace to those gathered inside. There is no need to be frightened. The assembled—men, women, and perhaps even children—are stunned and then overjoyed when they recognize the risen Jesus! They all share in the invitation to examine Jesus, to probe his wounds. They know with certainty that Jesus has conquered the grave. Everyone except Thomas, that is, who for some reason is not with the others that night.

The believers gather again the following Sunday evening; again the doors are locked from fear or prudence. This time Thomas is among them. Thomas knows that the others say they have seen the Lord, but he has told them that he will believe only when he sees the risen Jesus and has the same opportunity for attestation himself. And then suddenly, without warning, Jesus is the room. The doors are locked but he comes. He greets them, then speaks directly to Thomas. Come. Examine me. Stop doubting and believe. And he does. But Thomas comes to faith without having to probe and prod the body of Jesus. He comes to faith when he sees Jesus and exclaims, "My Lord and my God!" Whatever doubts he might have carried are abandoned. Thomas is not a doubter but the first apostle to proclaim the heartfelt certainty of his faith. So in the end this passage tells a story of faith. We honor Thomas for his proclamation this week.

══════════════ *Meditatio* ══════════════

"Do not be unbelieving, but believe." These words are addressed to Thomas a week after Jesus rose from the grave. John wants his church to know that Jesus appeared to all of the apostles. Where was Thomas the previous week? We will never know. But he stayed in contact with the others, and now they all gather again.

Take a few moments to put yourself in Thomas's place. Six days and nights will pass before you gather with the others, once again in fear and behind locked doors. Imagine the anticipation, the trepidation, the wonder, and the thoughts that are coursing through his mind. Would Jesus appear? What will Jesus say to him if he does? How would he respond? He has expressed doubt over the testimony of the others. But over the course of that week more and more men and women had reported similar experiences. There were the two disciples on the road to Emmaus who met the risen Jesus; St. Paul reminds us that Jesus appeared to many people, even to over 500 in a single visit (1 Corinthians 15:1–7). It does not take much to imagine that any doubts he had are fading as hope grows in his heart. Then Thomas meets the risen Lord himself. Jesus stands before him and invites him to come closer and examine his resurrected body. But there is no need. Thomas stands before Jesus, stunned. All he can do is exclaim, "My Lord and my God!" It is the perfect response, the appropriate statement of belief in the risen Jesus, then and now.

Oratio

Our prayer response is taken from the story. Thomas actually declines the invitation to examine the wounds of Jesus, and his exclamation of faith will be our prayer response as well. "My Lord and my God!"

Contemplatio

The last two verses of the reading this week bring the Gospel of John to an end. The chapter that follows (chapter 21) is added by our author at a later date. This week John reminds the church that he writes so we may believe that Jesus is both the Christ—the descendant of King David who is the Messiah—and that Jesus is also the Son of God. Jesus is man and God. Jesus is God and man. If we believe this, we will have life in his name.

Thomas becomes the example of that sort of believer. Jesus encourages him for believing because of what he sees, but stresses to the apostles that even more blessed will be those who have not seen the risen Jesus yet believe. That accounts for you and me! Unless you have had a personal vision of the Lord, you and I came to faith in a similar manner. It was because of what we heard, and that was the gospel, the good news of salvation read and explained to us on a weekly basis. In his letter to the Romans, Paul writes that "faith comes from what is heard, and what is heard comes through the word of Christ" (Romans 10:17). Pray for the person who will preach the Word in the church you attend. Pray specifically that this preached Word will transform those who hear it and help bring forth spiritual fruit in our lives.

OTHER READINGS: ACTS 5:12–16; REVELATION 1:9–11a, 12–13, 17–19

THIRD SUNDAY OF EASTER

YOU FOLLOW ME

JOHN 21:1-19

¹ After this, Jesus revealed himself again to his disciples at the Sea of Tiberias. He revealed himself in this way. ² Together were Simon Peter, Thomas called Didymus, Nathanael from Cana in Galilee, Zebedee's sons, and two others of his disciples. ³ Simon Peter said to them, "I am going fishing." They said to him, "We also will come with you." So they went out and got into the boat, but that night they caught nothing. ⁴ When it was already dawn, Jesus was standing on the shore; but the disciples did not realize that it was Jesus. ⁵ Jesus said to them, "Children, have you caught anything to eat?" They answered him, "No." ⁶ So he said to them, "Cast the net over the right side of the boat and you will find something." So they cast it, and were not able to pull it in because of the number of fish. ⁷ So the disciple whom Jesus loved said to Peter, "It is the Lord." When Simon Peter heard that it was the Lord, he tucked in his garment, for he was lightly clad, and jumped into the sea. ⁸ The other disciples came in the boat, for they were not far from shore, only about a hundred yards, dragging the net with the fish. ⁹ When they climbed out on shore, they saw a charcoal fire with fish on it and bread.

¹⁰ Jesus said to them, "Bring some of the fish you just caught." ¹¹ So Simon Peter went over and dragged the net ashore full of one hundred fifty-three large fish. Even though there were so many, the net was not torn. ¹² Jesus said to them, "Come, have breakfast." And none of the disciples dared to ask him, "Who are you?" because they realized it was the Lord. ¹³ Jesus came over and took the bread and gave it to them, and in like manner the fish. ¹⁴ This was now the third time Jesus was revealed to his disciples after being raised from the dead.

¹⁵ When they had finished breakfast, Jesus said to Simon Peter, "Simon, son of John, do you love me more than these?" He said to him, "Yes, Lord, you know that I love you." He said to him, "Feed my lambs." ¹⁶ He then said to him a second time, "Simon, son of John, do you love me?" He said to him, "Yes, Lord, you know that I love you." He said to him, "Tend my sheep." ¹⁷ He said to him the third time, "Simon, son of John, do you love me?" Peter was distressed that he had said to him a third time, "Do you love me?" and he said to him, "Lord, you know everything; you know that I love you." [Jesus] said to him, "Feed my sheep. ¹⁸ Amen, amen, I say to you, when you were younger, you used to dress yourself and go where you wanted; but when you grow old, you will stretch out your hands, and someone else will dress you and lead you where you do not want to go." ¹⁹ He said this signifying by what kind of death he would glorify God. And when he had said this, he said to him, "Follow me."

Lectio

John 21 is a story the Evangelist added to the end of the original Gospel. In the last verse of the prior chapter, John says Jesus did "many other things," but he is not sure the whole world could contain the books that would have to be written to recount them! This week we meet the resurrected Jesus along the shoreline of the Sea of Galilee near the commercial fishing village of Capernaum. A group of the apostles have gathered in this familiar setting in anticipation of his arrival. Peter, the leader of the group, says that he is going to go fishing. The others come along, boarding boats to spend what turns out to be a fruitless night.

John reminds us that commercial fishing on the Sea of Galilee is always done in the nighttime hours. The best fishing grounds are in the lake's northeast quadrant, near the village of Bethsaida. Fishing boats sail out from Capernaum with the favorable evening breezes, then row back in the early morning calm. As they return this morning, the disciples see Jesus standing on the shore, but they don't recognize him.

They still have some distance to row when Jesus speaks. His voice carries across the open bay. He notes they must not have had any success since their boats are riding too high in the water. Jesus suggests that they cast their nets a final time. Perhaps they will find fish nearer to shore. Why would seasoned fishermen follow the advice of a man on shore? Peter and his companions know that the fishing grounds near Capernaum have been fished out for years. Perhaps the man can see a school of fish near the boats. Still, what harm is there in one more cast? Suddenly their nets capture so many fish they can't handle them.

The "disciple whom Jesus loved," usually identified as John the Evangelist, now recognizes Jesus. Had he remembered another time that Jesus directed Peter to cast his nets into the same familiar waters (Luke 5:1–11)? The miracle has happened again! While it's John who recognizes Jesus, it's Peter who hears his exclamation and jumps into the shallow water, leaving the younger John and the others to secure the great catch (they have been commercial fishermen after all, and it feels too valuable to release).

Jesus shares a meal with the disciples and afterward calls Peter aside. As they walk, Jesus asks Peter three questions. Each is intended to discern the level of dedication Peter has toward Jesus and to invite him to leadership among the apostles. Do you love me, Peter? These are questions about Peter's loyalty to Jesus, for "love" in this culture means to be attached or connected to another person. Three times Jesus asks Peter if he loves him. Three times Peter responds that he does.

Jesus commissions Peter to feed the lambs, to care for the sheep, and to feed the mature animals as well. Peter's threefold denial of Jesus in the courtyard of the high priest is now addressed. Peter will feed the lambs, the new believers. Peter will care for the sheep as they grow; he is to shepherd the flock. Finally, Peter will feed the mature sheep, guiding them in the paths to follow to find verdant pasture and fresh water. He is to shepherd Jesus's flock, the church.

The scene ends with words of prophecy. Jesus reveals that Peter will die an untimely death. Others will lead him where he will not want to go. Peter will follow in the footsteps of Jesus, and indeed we learn from history that Peter dies a martyr, crucified in Rome, a victim of the same death sentence as the Lord.

Meditatio

What is the intention of the Evangelist in recording that 153 fish were caught that morning? If there is a symbolic meaning behind the number it is hard to discern. My take is that it reveals the tendency of commercial fisherman to know the number and value of their catch. Fishing nets capture many kinds of fish, but only certain types (those with fins and scales) can be taken to market. Peter and John's professional minds would remember vividly that valuable catch—which would now be left behind so that they can again respond to Jesus's call to follow.

The earlier story in Luke 5 with a similar miracle ends with the invitation to Peter, Andrew, James, and John to leave their nets and follow Jesus. After this encounter, Jesus invites these same men to follow him. They do.

Our Gospel this week reminds us of our own initial call. Now we have a fresh invitation to follow Jesus. Sometimes we, like these disciples, need to be invited again (and again, and again?) into active participation in ministry and service to others. Peter and the others who fished all night will once again leave behind a large and valuable catch to follow Jesus.

Oratio

I found a "Fishers of Men" prayer that will help us this week as we prepare to hear the Gospel proclaimed in our churches this weekend.

Father God, I want the hands of a true fisher of men. Lord, help us not to be afraid to go wherever the fish are. Let us not be afraid to get our hands dirty. Father help us not to just "catch and release" new converts; let us also be disciplers of men as well. In Jesus's name we pray, Amen.

The Gospel ends with Jesus inviting Peter to follow him immediately after he reveals to him how he will die. Jesus wants Peter first to return with him to the fire and to the other disciples. He will continue his training until they all return to Jerusalem in advance of the celebration of Pentecost.

The words "follow me" work on a different level as we imagine what our action response might be this week. Take a few moments to recall any memories of times when Jesus asked you to follow him into a situation you thought would be fraught with peril. I hope that your memory is not as challenging as Peter's prophecy. Still, as the good shepherd, Jesus must lead the flock through the "valley of the shadow of death" if the animals he cares for are going to find the rich pastures on the heights above. The flock moves forward, confident that the shepherd can protect them from predation with his rod and staff (Psalm 23). *Follow me.* Where, Lord? These two words of invitation are enough for our contemplation this week.

OTHER READINGS: ACTS 5:27–32, 40b–41; REVELATION 5:11–14

FOURTH SUNDAY OF EASTER

AMONG HIS SHEEP

JOHN 10:27–30

[27] "My sheep hear my voice; I know them, and they follow me. [28] I give them eternal life, and they shall never perish. No one can take them out of my hand. [29] My Father, who has given them to me, is greater than all, and no one can take them out of the Father's hand. [30] The Father and I are one."

We need context for this week's brief Gospel reading. We are in the middle of John 10, a chapter where Jesus tells his disciples that he is the "good shepherd," willing to lay down his life for his sheep. He is building on a familiar biblical image. David famously speaks of God as his shepherd in Psalm 23 and the prophet Ezekiel speaks of God as the good shepherd who courageously searches for his lost sheep until they are found (Ezekiel 34). Jesus here presents himself as this shepherd. His sheep—his disciples—follow because they recognize his voice. They will not follow the voice of a stranger.

This ability of sheep to respond to the voice of one shepherd is well attested. In the Middle East, small flocks are often penned together in larger groups for the night. There is safety in numbers and the animals quickly quiet down and can rest undisturbed without fear of predators. At dawn the shepherd arrives at the community pen and opens the gate. He then employs a series of unique sounds and whistles that his animals recognize and respond to, so calling out his sheep from the larger flock. I have witnessed this myself. No one challenges the shepherd. Everyone knows that only his sheep will answer his summons.

The religious leaders in the time of Jesus were not shepherds themselves and so seem not to understand Jesus's use of this metaphor (perhaps willfully so). They have become frustrated and demand that if Jesus is the Messiah, he should say so plainly (John 10:24). Jesus responds. He reminds them of the works—the miracles—he has accomplished in his Father's name that reveal his identity. The evidence is clear to his disciples but not to these leaders because they "are not among my sheep" (verse 26).

Our Gospel begins in the midst of this engagement, which is set on the grounds of the temple itself. Jesus says again that his sheep recognize his voice and follow him. They are not going to stay in the pen any longer. He will lead them out. They will not respond to the voice of outsiders—that is, the temple leadership. Jesus will give them eternal life. They will have everything a sheep needs to be happy and content. His flock belongs to God. Jesus states clearly that he and the Father are one. To see Jesus is to see the Father. If you know the one you know the other. In this way Jesus is the perfect Middle Eastern son. He is the exact image of the Father.

This statement is too much for these religious leaders to bear. Immediately after our reading, they quickly assemble and collect rocks, intending to stone Jesus. In their ears these words are blasphemy! They think that Jesus the man is claiming to be God! And he is.

Why do sheep and their behaviors captivate the biblical authors? In a pastoral setting, sheep are the flock animals the ancients associated with honor, unlike goats. Sheep do not cry out in the face of danger, slaughter, or shearing. They are silent and stoic. In Isaiah 53:7 we hear of the "suffering servant" who submits quietly to harsh treatment. He is compared with "a lamb led to slaughter" and "a sheep silent before shearers" who does not open his mouth in complaint. Male sheep are also honored for guarding their females from access by other males, unlike the shamefully profligate goats. Sheep are loyal and will not follow a voice they do not recognize. The preferred animal to offer as a sacrifice for the forgiveness of sin is a year-old, unblemished lamb (thus John the Baptist refers to Jesus as the "Lamb of God who takes away the sin of the world," John 1:29).

In our meditation this week consider your relationship with God as the shepherd caring for his flock. How has Jesus been the good shepherd in your life? You might find Psalm 23 useful as a template for your meditation. Read through the psalm and note how God has provided for you in the various ways a shepherd provides for each member of the flock. Jesus promises his disciples eternal life. By the end of the psalm, King David is confident that goodness and mercy will follow after him always and that he will dwell in the house of the Lord forever. Ask the Lord for that same confident assurance for yourself this week.

———— *Oratio* ————

The first few verses of Psalm 23 serve well this week as our prayer response to the Gospel. Ask God to show you how this is true for you.

"The LORD is my shepherd; there is nothing I lack. In green pastures he makes me lie down; to still waters he leads me; he restores my soul. He guides me along right paths for the sake of his name."

———— *Contemplatio* ————

"My sheep hear my voice; I know them, and they follow me." How do you hear the voice of Jesus? Where do you hear the voice of Jesus? How has Jesus revealed himself to you so that you recognize and continue to follow him? Take a moment to ponder these questions. Do you hear his voice in church? In your quiet time of prayer? When you are listening to specific music? Do you hear his voice in nature, in the power of the storm or in the gentle patter of rain? Does Jesus speak to you when you fellowship with family and friends? Try to identify times and situations so that in the future, when it seems he is not speaking, you will know how to get to a place where you can hear his voice again. Then ask the Lord to speak to you in new ways so that your spiritual ears stay tuned to the sure and gentle call of the good shepherd.

OTHER READINGS: ACTS 13:14, 43–52; REVELATION 7:9, 14b–17

FIFTH SUNDAY OF EASTER

COMMANDED TO A NEW FAMILY

JOHN 13:31–33a, 34–35

[31] When he had left, Jesus said, "Now is the Son of Man glorified, and God is glorified in him. [32] [If God is glorified in him,] God will also glorify him in himself, and he will glorify him at once. [33] My children, I will be with you only a little while longer.... [34] I give you a new commandment: love one another. As I have loved you, so you also should love one another. [35] This is how all will know that you are my disciples, if you have love for one another."

Lectio

As is often the case we need to place this week's Gospel passage in context. We are with Jesus and his disciples at the Last Supper. In the middle of the proceedings Jesus has surprised everyone as he stands up, ties a towel around his waist, and washes their feet. Jesus tells them this is a model they are to remember and repeat. This kind of servant leadership will be expected from those who serve in the company of Jesus.

Jesus then predicts his betrayal, identifying Judas and sending him from the upper room. Our Gospel account begins here. "When he had

Be Vigilant! Lectio Divina for Year C

left" refers to the departure of Judas into the night. We assume he leaves to collect a guard cohort that will return to arrest Jesus (and the others?). Time is short. Jesus knows he has a few precious moments with his disciples before they will be forced to vacate the premises.

Jesus says that "now" the Son of Man is glorified, and God is glorified in him. "Son of Man" is the title from Daniel 7:13–14 that Jesus uses to identify himself as the promised Messiah. Another translation of "glorified" is "honored." The Son of Man is "honored" and God the Father will be "honored" by him as an obedient son. Honor is the central value in the Middle East—personal, familial, and corporate. It is a public claim to value and worth together with a public acknowledgment of the claim. One's goal in life was to retain honor and avoid shame. An honorable son or daughter brought joy to their parents. Jesus is honored by God because he is an obedient son—and his obedience meant death on the cross (see Philippians 2:8–11). Jesus knows that the departure of Judas means that the events that will lead to the cross are imminent.

Since he has only a little more time with them, Jesus gives the disciples a new commandment. Everything is about to change. Until now they all had a particular attachment to Jesus. Now they are called to something more. They are called to love one another.

———————————— *Meditatio* ————————————

"I give you a new commandment: love one another." How is this commandment new? Jesus is teaching us about the primacy of love. The word is perhaps best defined as "attachment," conveying the biblical meaning of staying connected to others. Jesus has taught those who follow him that they will have to love their enemies by doing good to those who hate them. Likewise, Jesus teaches those who would follow him that they will have to hate (detach from) their fathers and mothers and love him if they want to continue as his disciples. But still, why is the commandment in this week's passage new?

The commandment to love one another, when lived out in the church, will be tangible evidence to everyone else of the presence of authentic followers of Jesus. How will this be accomplished? Jesus wants the disciples to become a new family consisting of all the disciples who relate to one another as brothers and sisters from this point forward. The followers of Jesus—eventually Jews and Greeks, slaves and free persons, men and women—all will be part of the single family of God. They will be the church, the *ecclesia,* the ones called out of the world. Older family, racial, national, and group loyalties will fall by the way. A new ethic will be revealed to the world. The followers of Jesus hear a new commandment: to love one another. They are challenged to relate to each other from now on as family members.

When you decide to follow Jesus you become a member of a new family—and family comes first. Members of your new family will care for and love you. Others will see this expression of family-based love and will want to be part of it too. Are our faith communities revealing this kind of family love? Are we relating to each other in the church as our brothers and sisters? As our fathers and mothers? As members of the family of God? Take a moment to meditate on these questions this week.

Oratio

In 1 Corinthians 13:4–8a the apostle Paul describes what familial love should look like in the church. We will use his insights on love in our prayer response this week, asking God to make this kind of love true among us.

"Love is patient, love is kind. It is not jealous, is not pompous, it is not inflated, it is not rude, it does not seek its own interests, it is not quick-tempered, it does not brood over injury, it does not rejoice over wrongdoing but rejoices with the truth. It bears all things, believes all things, hopes all things, and endures all things. Love never fails."

Contemplatio

Family and faith now go hand in hand. When we as members of the church relate to each other as part of the family of faith, people outside take notice. This witness is compelling. This is how the world will know that we belong to Jesus and have been born again. We have to learn how to love one another as family members and not as strangers who gather during the same religious service each week.

In the Middle East family comes first. The church is the new family that these disciples must call their own. They have left everything and everyone to follow Jesus. Now they are being called by Jesus to love one another as they had previously loved and honored members of their immediate family group. We too are disciples of Jesus and as such are destined to live as a new family. Church members living as a family are a powerful witness that Jesus is ushering something new into the world. Pray this week that your church community recognizes this call to family and in so doing is revealed as a witness of Jesus and the power of his resurrection.

OTHER READINGS: ACTS 14:21-27; REVELATION 21:1-5a

SIXTH SUNDAY OF EASTER

MY PEACE I GIVE TO YOU

JOHN 14:23-29

²³ Jesus answered and said to him, "Whoever loves me will keep my word, and my Father will love him, and we will come to him and make our dwelling with him. ²⁴ Whoever does not love me does not keep my words; yet the word you hear is not mine but that of the Father who sent me.

²⁵ "I have told you this while I am with you. ²⁶ The Advocate, the holy Spirit that the Father will send in my name—he will teach you everything and remind you of all that [I] told you. ²⁷ Peace I leave with you; my peace I give to you. Not as the world gives do I give it to you. Do not let your hearts be troubled or afraid. ²⁸ You heard me tell you, 'I am going away and I will come back to you.' If you loved me, you would rejoice that I am going to the Father; for the Father is greater than I. ²⁹ And now I have told you this before it happens, so that when it happens you may believe."

—— *Lectio* ——

The Gospel passage opens in the middle of a chapter dedicated to the promise of the Holy Spirit. This Advocate or Paraclete will be given to the disciples after the resurrection event. Before our Gospel opens we note that Judas has been identified as a traitor and has been dismissed by Jesus to carry out his plan. The Passover meal will come to an unexpected end when Jesus tells his disciples at the end of this same chapter that they will be leaving the upper room in haste and before the meal formally concludes with the final cup of wine called "the cup of acceptance." They have to vacate the upper room in anticipation of Judas returning with a guard to arrest Jesus. They will soon be on the move.

Jesus reminds his disciples that if they love him they will keep his commandments. Love is understood to be a pragmatic expression of attachment. If you love someone you remain attached and loyal to that individual. Jesus knows the disciples love him and then promises them that he will ask the Father to send them another "advocate" to be with them always (see John 14:16ff). Jesus calls this Advocate the "spirit of truth" that the world cannot accept. Jesus reminds them that this "Advocate" has been with them while he has been their Rabbi and that this new "Spirit" will be "in" them soon (John 14:16). Jesus says he will not leave them orphans. He will come back to them in a new form, as the new Spirit that he promises will guide and direct their teaching and remind them of all that he has taught them over the three years of his public ministry.

Jesus will not be physically present any longer. He will come to them through the promised Spirit. An *advocate* is defined as "one who stands by the side of the defendant." The advocate is a court official who would plead the case of the defendant before a tribunal or judge. He would provide the evidence needed to gain freedom for the client based on his expert skills in the courts of the day. The Holy Spirit promised to the disciples will function in a similar manner. The Advocate is the truth-telling agent of God who will inspire and direct the lives of the believer. The Advocate sent from the Father will teach them everything and remind the disciples of all that they had been told. Their training as disciples will be completed when they experience this indwelling of the Holy Spirit on the evening after the resurrection and even more fully on the Feast of Pentecost.

Before they leave the upper room Jesus promises the disciples his peace, his Shalom from God. That holy peace will come upon them when the

Advocate is welcomed in their lives. Jesus counsels them not to worry, not to be troubled or afraid. They will each receive this Spirit when the events of the passion are complete. Jesus even expects the disciples to rejoice in the fact that he is going leave them to rejoin his Father, because his departure allows the Father the opportunity to send them the Holy Spirit in return. The Advocate is on the way.

And now they are off. It is time to leave the upper room and make their way through the city and across the temple mount. They will exit the city and find their way into the olive grove called Gethsemane. Judas is also on the move and Jesus needs to get ahead of the guard that he has hastily assembled. That is why the chapter ends with the words of Jesus, "Get up, let us go." He still has a great deal to teach them along the way.

Meditatio

"Whoever loves me will keep my word, and my Father will love him, and we will come to him and make our dwelling with him." What are we to make of these words Jesus spoke to his disciples that night in the upper room? Love is an action word that demands a decision followed by activity. That decision to act and following through in the normal course of our lives reveals the depth of our commitment to the Lord. If the disciples truly love Jesus they will keep his word by living according to his teaching.

Jesus has revealed himself to be the new Moses. Do you recall his teaching style in delivering the Sermon on the Mount? "You have heard it said … but I say to you …" Jesus affirms the teaching of Moses and then takes his disciples to the next level. Moses taught that we are not to kill. Jesus takes us deeper. He teaches that if you harbor anger in your heart you have already started the journey down a path that could lead to murder. Be mindful of the process, not just the final result. Learn to nip the process in the bud before thoughts give way to actions.

We dedicate our lives to live according to his teachings by the actions that demonstrate our faith. Jesus and the Father take up their dwelling within us. We become the new temple of God in the world. The Jerusalem temple was the house of God, but it was destined for destruction. The new temple of God is in the hearts and mind of each believer. The evidence of

God alive and active in the world is the lives of Christian men and women who live out of God's life and follow his teachings. This is how we can share a peace in the world that the world cannot give.

--- *Oratio* ---

"Come Holy Spirit, fill the hearts of your faithful and kindle within them the fire of your love. Send forth your Spirit and they shall be created. And you shall renew the face of the earth."

--- *Contemplatio* ---

Jesus promises to leave us the gift of peace, his *shalom,* a term that conveys the sense of wholeness when God is ever present and in charge of the concerns of men and women of faith. The world cannot provide anyone this profound *shalom.* At best it can offer periods of relative calm, not what Jesus promises, a true and active peace that "surpasses all understanding."

Julian of Norwich was a saint and Christian mystic. One of her most memorable sayings is, "All shall be well, and all shall be well, and all manner of thing shall be well." The saint's saying captures the meaning behind the kind of peace Jesus promises us in the Gospel. Take this to heart as you prepare for worship. The peace we know as Christians is a gift from God. When we experience that unique *shalom* from heaven we gain the spiritual confidence that in the end all will be well, and all shall be well, and all manner of thing shall be well.

OTHER READINGS: ACTS 15:1–2, 22–29; REVELATION 21:10–14, 22–23

SEVENTH SUNDAY OF EASTER

PERFECTION AS ONE

JOHN 17:20–26

20 "I pray not only for them, but also for those who will believe in me through their word, 21 so that they may all be one, as you, Father, are in me and I in you, that they also may be in us, that the world may believe

that you sent me. ²² And I have given them the glory you gave me, so that they may be one, as we are one, ²³ I in them and you in me, that they may be brought to perfection as one, that the world may know that you sent me, and that you loved them even as you loved me. ²⁴ Father, they are your gift to me. I wish that where I am they also may be with me, that they may see my glory that you gave me, because you loved me before the foundation of the world. ²⁵ Righteous Father, the world also does not know you, but I know you, and they know that you sent me. ²⁶ I made known to them your name and I will make it known, that the love with which you loved me may be in them and I in them."

Lectio

Our reading this week is from a story that is unique to the Fourth Gospel. The Evangelist remembers the journey of Jesus and the apostles as they leave the upper room to stay ahead of Judas's plan to have Jesus arrested. The Gospel of John devotes four chapters (14–17) to the events and teachings of this journey across the city and out Jerusalem's Golden Gate to the olive grove called Gethsemane on the eastern flank of the Mount of Olives.

The Gospel opens in the middle of a scene with Jesus in prayer. He lifts his eyes to the heavens—and we can be confident his hands as well—as he stands before the temple, the house of God on earth. His prayer is the content of this entire chapter. He has prayed, "Father, the hour has come. Give glory to your son, so that your son may glorify you" (John 17:1). The word *glory* used in our English translation may not fully capture the Greek, the sense of which seems more focused on honor. Jesus prays that his Father will honor him as his Son because of his obedience, and that his obedience will be a sign of the way he will honor his Father. Jesus knows well what horrors await him at Calvary, but he will still press on to complete the work the Father has asked him to accomplish (John 17:4). He is the new Isaac who will allow himself to be bound by his Father and offered as a sacrifice without cry or complaint.

In verses 6–19 Jesus prays for his apostles, the ones he has known and trained. He prays that they will remain loyal to one another in this imminent time of crisis. He reminds the Father that he has always protected them from harm. He reveals that he is going to return to the Father, clearing the path for his disciples to make that same journey in the future.

Now we arrive at our reading. Jesus continues to pray, not only for the apostles with him but also for all of those who will believe in him because of the words of the apostles. He prays that all who respond to the invitation through their preaching will share the same unity that Jesus shares with his Father. This Spirit-inspired unity will be a witness to the world that cannot be denied. We know that the agent of this supernatural unity will be the indwelling Holy Spirit, who will come on Pentecost.

Our reading ends at the conclusion of Jesus's "great high priestly prayer." Jesus prays that the "love with which you loved me may be in them and I in them" too. That love is Jesus's awareness that he is attached and dedicated to his Father and his Father's will. Jesus prays that his followers will be connected to each other as Jesus is connected to his Father. This love for one another will be the hallmark of the new family of faith, the church. This witness of unity will be a source of wonder and amazement and will be a central pillar in the efforts of the apostles to take the message of the gospel the ends of the earth.

––––––––––––––––––––––––––––––––– *Meditatio* –––––––––––––––––––––––––––––––––

Jesus prays this week for future believers who will come to faith as a result of the preached word. Jesus prays that they—we—will be brought to "perfection" in our unity (verse 23) so that the world will know that Jesus was sent by the Father, and that God the Father will love the followers of Jesus—you and me—just like he loves Jesus.

How can our unity as believers be brought to "perfection"? That seems a tall order when we consider our sinful natures and the effects of temptation in our lives. In Matthew 5:48 Jesus says that his followers are to "be perfect, just as your heavenly Father is perfect." Is this really possible? The Greek term includes the concept of "mature." To be perfect in this biblical sense means to be whole, grown up, and complete. Followers of Jesus are to grow to maturity, to completeness in Christ. The apostle Paul understood this, for example as he criticizes the members of the Corinthian church of not growing into maturity. (1 Corinthians 3:1–3; 14:20).

Our meditation reminds us to grow up in the Lord, to be brought to perfection by striving to become mature men and women of faith. Our maturity will be expressed in our unity, our attachment to each other in our faith communities. Such attachment is a powerful witness to a fractured and fragmented world. The world divides, but faith unites. The love we share with one another, and the faith we have in common, is our focus this week.

<hr>

Oratio

1 Corinthians 13 is the great love chapter in the New Testament. We will remember these words of St. Paul as we pray to be attached to others and for guidance in expressing our love in action: "If I speak in human and angelic tongues but do not have love, I am a resounding gong or a clashing cymbal. And if I have the gift of prophecy and comprehend all mysteries and all knowledge; if I have all faith so as to move mountains but do not have love, I am nothing.... So faith, hope, love remain, these three; but the greatest of these is love" (1 Corinthians 13:1–2, 13).

<hr>

Contemplatio

Jesus prays for those who will believe because they will hear the word preached by his disciples. Many of us are the direct answer to this prayer. If you are like me, you came to faith in Jesus because a great preacher taught you the Word of God with authority and conviction. In my life that man is a Dominican priest, Fr. Tom DeMan, pastor at the Newman Center at Arizona State University. In college, I often attended events and services Fr. Tom presided over. His love of and attention to the Word in his preaching changed the course of my life. I rededicated my life to Jesus in that community and have been growing in my love of the Word ever since.

Take a few moments this week on the way to the church service of your choice and pray for the person who will be delivering the sermon that day. Ask the Father to send the Spirit upon that person so that the words spoken in the service will convince others that Jesus is truly the way, the truth, and the life.

OTHER READINGS: ACTS 7:55–60; REVELATION 22:12–14, 16–17, 20

MIGHTY ACTS OF GOD

ACTS 2:1-12

¹ When the time for Pentecost was fulfilled, they were all in one place together. ² And suddenly there came from the sky a noise like a strong driving wind, and it filled the entire house in which they were. ³ Then there appeared to them tongues as of fire, which parted and came to rest on each one of them. ⁴ And they were all filled with the holy Spirit and began to speak in different tongues, as the Spirit enabled them to proclaim.

⁵ Now there were devout Jews from every nation under heaven staying in Jerusalem. ⁶ At this sound, they gathered in a large crowd, but they were confused because each one heard them speaking in his own language. ⁷ They were astounded, and in amazement they asked, "Are not all these people who are speaking Galileans? ⁸ Then how does each of us hear them in his own native language? ⁹ We are Parthians, Medes, and Elamites, inhabitants of Mesopotamia, Judea and Cappadocia, Pontus and Asia, ¹⁰ Phrygia and Pamphylia, Egypt and the districts of Libya near Cyrene, as well as travelers from Rome, ¹¹ both Jews and converts to Judaism, Cretans and Arabs, yet we hear them speaking in our own tongues of the mighty acts of God." ¹² They were all astounded and bewildered, and said to one another, "What does this mean?"

———————————— *Lectio* ————————————

The church celebrates its birthday on Sunday as we gather for the feast of Pentecost, remembering the morning when the Holy Spirit appeared as "tongues of fire" on 120 disciples gathered and praying in the upper room in Jerusalem. The events recorded in Acts 2 bring new significance to a Jewish feast celebrating the giving of the Law. Fifty days after their miraculous deliverance from Egyptian captivity at the Red Sea, the people of Israel gather at the foot of Mount Sinai. God speaks to the assembly from the mountain, giving them the ten brief statements—Christians will later call them the Ten Commandments—in a voice heard by every man, woman, and child. The event inspires awe and wonder, and many who hear God speak respond with fright (see Exodus 20:18–22).

In Jesus's time Pentecost was one three annual pilgrimage festivals (along with Passover and Tabernacles) that brought tens of thousands to the temple. The pilgrims Luke identifies as "devout" that day are considered particularly holy because they made the long journey to Jerusalem for Passover and also stayed the additional fifty days to celebrate the giving of the Law. It is a time of communal celebration, a time to eat and drink, to honor the God who was faithful in delivering his people from captivity and making them a nation. They recall God speaking from the holy mountain and his ongoing speech through his Word.

The disciples are gathered because Jesus has directed them to stay in Jerusalem "until you are clothed with power from on high" (Luke 24:49). That was ten days ago. They knew enough to anticipate *something* wonderful at the great feast of Pentecost. They would not disappointed. They are assembled at the time when a lamb is sacrificed in the temple on behalf of the people. From the vantage point of the upper room they could hear and see something of the proceedings on the other side of the city.

A large crowd is gathered on the temple mount when the morning calm is broken by the sound of a rushing wind. It draws many curious people to the scene. They follow the sounds of men and women engaged in loud and ecstatic praise of God. Entering the large upper room, the crowd is amazed to hear dozens of people speaking of the mighty acts of God in languages that they should not know. Where had people from Galilee learned to speak any of the fifteen languages that mark this group of pilgrims from across the Roman Empire? Some have even come from Cyrene, more than eight hundred miles away in what is modern Libya!

Luke records that they are collectively "astounded," "amazed," and "bewildered." What does this mean? Peter speaks on behalf of the others to answer that question in his sermon that will follow. In the meantime the pilgrims witness the reversal of Babel. In Genesis 11 the common language of the world was confused. Now everyone hears the message clearly. The mighty acts of God are remembered because that same mighty God is on the move again.

After the Spirit descends those gathered in the upper room each begin to speak of the "mighty acts of God." In the Jewish context, "mighty acts of God" usually evokes nine specific memories of God acting on behalf of his people as protector and advocate. Those filled with the Spirit are heard in fifteen different languages recalling great historical events that begin with the narrative of creation, followed by God choosing the ancient fathers of Israel (Abraham, Isaac, Jacob). Then on to the Exodus story and their collective deliverance from slavery, then God speaking to the people from Mount Sinai. The stories about the wilderness wandering and forty years of miraculous provision qualify as mighty acts, as does the gift of Canaan as a homeland, of God establishing a monarchy, and of King David securing Jerusalem as a center for worship and the site of the temple. During this time they would also remember the many and varied voices of the prophets God spoke through to guide and direct the nation.

These are the classic nine mighty acts that God accomplished for his people even before Jesus came. What mighty acts are yet to come? That is the key question to ask yourself this week.

Another question to consider is what this means for you. If you were filled with the Spirit, what "mighty acts of God" would you proclaim? What has God done for you that would qualify as a "mighty act"? Does any event or experience come to mind? Recall times that God broke through to reveal the power of his Spirit to transform and provide meaning in your life. I invite you to pray with me that we will be open to God acting in our lives today, this week, and in the years that will follow.

This prayer was composed by Brother Roger of the Taizé Community in France and captures the essence of the Pentecost event for us this week.

"Living God, you want us to have hearts that are completely simple, to the point that the complicated things in life do not bring us to a halt. Through the Holy Spirit, the spirit of the Risen Christ, you come to open a way for us, a way that is possible; on it we understand that you love us first, before we loved you."

Action response: Pray that the Holy Spirit will come upon you like those in the upper room. "Astounded" and "bewildered" are adjectives Luke uses to describe the response of those present. We can also say that those filled with the Spirit and speaking other languages were also "amazed" and "filled with wonder." The witnesses could not make sense of what they saw and heard. It was new, unexpected, powerful—and a bit frightening.

"Astounded" and "bewildered." "Amazed" and "filled with wonder." On the one hand the believers knew that God was in the mix and that this new Spirit had been sent from heaven. But what did it mean? How were they to go forward from here? It would take time to process. The same holds true for us. When God sends the Spirit, things change. We are allowed to wonder what it all means. Why me, Lord? Why now, Lord? Where now, Lord? When we open ourselves to the Spirit, transformation takes place that will not leave us the same person we were before. The Spirit speaks to us. The Spirit appeared as "tongues of fire" and the disciples found themselves proclaiming the mighty acts of God. Trust God this week. Remember God's mighty acts in your life and pray for a fresh outpouring of the Spirit. Be ready to be as astounded and bewildered, as amazed and filled with wonder, as the believers in the upper room.

OTHER READINGS: 1 CORINTHIANS 12:3b–7, 12–13; JOHN 14:15–16, 23b–26

THE MOST HOLY TRINITY

UNITED

JOHN 16:12-15

¹² "I have much more to tell you, but you cannot bear it now. ¹³ But when he comes, the Spirit of truth, he will guide you to all truth. He will not speak on his own, but he will speak what he hears, and will declare to you the things that are coming. ¹⁴ He will glorify me, because he will take from what is mine and declare it to you. ¹⁵ Everything that the

Father has is mine; for this reason I told you that he will take from what is mine and declare it to you."

<hr>

Lectio

This week we celebrate the feast of the Most Holy Trinity. While the term "Trinity" does not appear in either Old or New Testaments it is a central doctrine that has united Christians since the time of Jesus. The Gospel reading opens in the middle of a conversation Jesus is having with the apostles as they make their way from the upper room across the upper city of Jerusalem toward the temple mount and on to the garden of Gethsemane, where he will wait for the group coming with Judas to arrest him.

Jesus tells them that only after he leaves them will he be able to send them the Advocate, the Comforter, the Paraclete—the Holy Spirit. Jesus calls this Advocate the "Spirit of truth," but what does that mean to those who hear the promise of Jesus that night?

Middle Eastern culture then and now operates on two opposing values, honor and shame. Life here is all about attaining and retaining honor while doing whatever it takes to avoid shame. Honor is far more valuable than money, so much more that it is hard to overestimate. This presents us with a problem. When a culture values honor this highly, men and women will be willing to lie, deceive, and keep secrets to preserve it. Peter, for example, lies to the servant girl in the courtyard of the high priest to preserve his personal honor. She is not a member of his immediate family so he does not owe her the truth. Peter's lie is to protect himself from guilt by his association with the prisoner Jesus.

The use of secrecy, deception, and lies in the Middle East can make life exasperating and hard to follow. How do you know when someone is telling the truth? The answer of Jesus is the promised appearance of the Advocate. The Spirit of truth will never speak on his own (he will never lie to protect honor) but will speak only what he hears from the Father. Jesus has said earlier in this teaching that he is here to glorify the Father (for example, John 14:13). Now Jesus promises that the Advocate will glorify him—that is, will honor Jesus—because he will assist in the final formation of the disciples. Everything that belongs to the Father belongs to the

Son, and the Advocate will dwell in the disciples to declare all of this to them! The Advocate will guide them into the way of truth in a culture that is often predicated on lies. Those who follow Jesus will not have to wonder about the truth any more. Jesus has promised the solution.

This explains why Jesus begins so many of his teachings with the phrase, "Amen, Amen, I say to you …" Jesus wants his followers to know that he is the way, the truth, and the life and that they can trust what he teaches them. There is no secrecy or deception in any of his words. They can trust him. When the Advocate comes they are to trust in him as well.

The promise of the coming Spirit was fulfilled in the upper room fifty days after the resurrection. The Evangelist this week reminds us that Jesus and the Father are one. They share the same mind and purpose, and they send the Advocate to make God's mind and purpose known to us. The Holy Spirit is the divine guide to all truth and will continue to guide and direct the church until the end.

—— *Meditatio* ——

What do we know about the Trinity? The church makes sense of the witness of the biblical writers and the startling claims of Jesus by teaching that God has revealed himself as three distinct persons with a single nature. I can understand this on a very basic level, for I am also three distinct persons with a single nature. I am the husband of my wife, the father of my children, and the grandfather of my grandchildren. My life is defined by these three distinct roles, each played by me: one individual person. This may not the best example, but it can help get us started.

The term "Trinity" is not in the Bible but the concept is present and clear. Take time to consider the importance of this doctrine in your life as a Christian. The Trinity is the central single doctrine that unites all who call themselves Christian. We are baptized into Christ's church with the Trinitarian formula of the Father, the Son, and the Holy Spirit. It can be a difficult doctrine to get our heads around, but its reality is witnessed when Christians are united with each other and support one another in prayer and service. That is the witness that the world needs to see more often, and the work that we need to participate in this week as we anticipate celebrating the feast of the Most Holy Trinity.

Psalm 143:10 provides our prayer response this week: "Teach me to do your will, for you are my God. May your kind spirit guide me on ground that is level."

One of the ways the Spirit leads us into all truth is by connecting our unique gifts and callings to build us together into the body of Christ. St. Paul teaches the Corinthians that there are different kinds of spiritual gifts, but each gift originates from the same Spirit (1 Corinthians 12:4). He maintains that each individual person in the church is given particular gifts that are intended to benefit others. We receive these spiritual gifts to share them in service! Someone in the church has the gift of wisdom, another has the gift of faith, still another the gift of encouragement, and another the gift of service. Each particular manifestation of the Spirit is intended for sharing so that God can use us to draw people to Jesus. What is your spiritual gift? The gift of the Holy Spirit that is unique to you? Where do you see the gifts of the Spirit manifested in your life? What spiritual gift are you sharing with the Body of Christ? Ask the Lord to reveal the spiritual gift that best suits you and pray for the grace to use that gift in service of others this week.

OTHER READINGS: PROVERBS 8:22–31; ROMANS 5:1–5

THE MOST HOLY BODY AND BLOOD OF CHRIST

GIVE THEM SOME FOOD YOURSELVES

LUKE 9:11b–17

[11] He received them and spoke to them about the kingdom of God, and he healed those who needed to be cured. [12] As the day was drawing to a close, the Twelve approached him and said, "Dismiss the crowd so that they can go to the surrounding villages and farms and find lodging and provisions; for we are in a deserted place here." [13] He said

to them, "Give them some food yourselves." They replied, "Five loaves and two fish are all we have, unless we ourselves go and buy food for all these people." [14] Now the men there numbered about five thousand. Then he said to his disciples, "Have them sit down in groups of [about] fifty." [15] They did so and made them all sit down. [16] Then taking the five loaves and the two fish, and looking up to heaven, he said the blessing over them, broke them, and gave them to the disciples to set before the crowd. [17] They all ate and were satisfied. And when the leftover fragments were picked up, they filled twelve wicker baskets.

Lectio

The Gospel story opens when the twelve apostles return to Capernaum after a brief internship of healing and preaching about the kingdom of God. Jesus has invited them to sail with him across the Sea of Galilee to a quiet spot near the fishing village of Bethsaida. Bethsaida was familiar to the disciples. In fact, as many as seven of the twelve apostles were born and raised in this village, located six miles from Capernaum near where the Jordan River flows into the larger lake. When the people of Capernaum watch the boats sail east they know the likely destination, and a crowd walks around the north shore of the lake to meet Jesus in Bethsaida.

When Jesus arrives he sees thousands of people gathered along the shoreline. He notes that they are like sheep without a shepherd and immediately gets out of the boat and begins to heal and preach to them about the kingdom of God. Eventually the afternoon draws to a close. His disciples counsel Jesus to send the crowds to the nearby villages to find food and lodging. Most in the crowd are observant Jews and would not carry food outside the kosher confines of a house. This was no picnic. They have no provisions with them. They need to purchase food that they can be assured is prepared under appropriate dietary restrictions.

Jesus offers the disciples another option. "Give them some food yourselves." But how? Where would they find enough food for thousands? In John's account of the event, Philip, one of the locals, tells Jesus that two hundred days wages would not purchase even a small amount for everyone (John 6:7). Jesus will multiply five fist-sized loaves of bread and two fish to feed five thousand men! In the Bible men are defined as males between the ages of 20 and 50. There were certainly males younger and older than this in the crowd as well as women and girls. It is quite possible that as many as ten thousand experienced the miracle of multiplication!

It is former fishermen who procure the five small barley loaves and two dried and salted fish for Jesus to offer to the crowd. This food was probably left over from the previous evening's fishing expedition. Galilean fisherman were considered ritually unclean since they had to handle "unclean" fish caught in their drift nets each night. Keeping kosher was not a paramount concern on their boats. Still, these loaves and fish are offered to Jesus, who gives thanks to God for this provision and then directs the apostles to distribute the food to the crowd. They do as directed, and when they are finished everyone present has eaten and is satisfied. They are so satisfied that the disciples are able to collect twelve baskets full of leftover fragments. Those wicker baskets were also sourced from the fishing boat, where they are used to sort fish after the night's haul.

What does this all mean? This is the only miracle recounted in all four Gospel accounts. In John's Gospel it is the springboard to the Bread of Life discourse in chapter 6. In the Old Testament the prophets Elijah and Elijah both multiplied bread, but not on the same scale as Jesus. Elisha multiplies twenty barley loaves to feed one hundred. Jesus multiplies five to feed five thousand! Jesus is greater than the prophets. Jesus is also greater than Moses. Moses called down manna from heaven and everyone ate until they were satisfied, but the manna did not last. There were no fragments left over to collect for later consumption. The manna would spoil by the next day, but not these loaves blessed and broken by Jesus. It is no wonder that in John's telling, the reaction of the crowd was a desire to make Jesus their king by force!

———————————— *Meditatio* ————————————

Why did Jesus use this opportunity to preach about the kingdom of God? What did he intend to convey about this kingdom? Jesus will reveal the true meaning of the kingdom at the Last Supper. In Luke 22:25–27 Jesus reminds the apostles that the kings of the Gentiles lord it over their subjects. Oppressive Roman authority figures insist on being addressed as "benefactors." This is not the model for anyone in a position of authority in the kingdom of God. Anyone who aspires to be the greatest in this kingdom will have to become the servant of all. Jesus has set this example for them. He leads as one who serves.

The crowds that followed Jesus must have been captivated by this sort of teaching of an approaching kingdom of God. This promised kingdom was antithetical to the hard Roman regime they knew. Jesus's teaching about this new kind of kingdom kept the crowds coming back for more.

Oratio

Let's pray Psalm 103:1–5. "Bless the LORD, my soul; all my being, bless his holy name! Bless the LORD, my soul; and do not forget all his gifts, who pardons all your sins, and heals all your ills, who redeems your life from the pit, and crowns you with mercy and compassion, who fills your days with good things, so your youth is renewed like the eagle's."

Contemplatio

Jesus takes the loaves and fishes and, looking up to heaven, "he said the blessing over them," broke them, and gave them to the disciples. They were charged to distribute the multiplied loaves and fish among the assembled masses. What was the blessing Jesus used? Was there a Jewish rite that applied? For a faithful Jew, all food that originates from the earth, like the small barley loaves and kosher species of fish (any fish with fins and scales) has no need to be blessed. These food items are "clean" already. So what is Jesus blessing that day?

Jesus raised his eyes to heaven to "bless the Lord" before the distribution of the miraculous provisions. To "bless the Lord" means to give thanks for all that has been provided. When Jesus does this, we are to understand that he is offering a prayer of thanks for all that God has provided.

We can do the same. Here is an action item to try this week. What follows is a change from the typical prayer we share before we eat a meal together as a family. Note the difference in the wording, which helps us focus on thanking the Lord for all that has been provided in our lives.

In place of the standard prayer, "Bless us, O Lord, and these your gifts, which we are about to receive from your bounty," try "We bless you, O Lord, for these gifts that we are about to receive, through Christ our Lord. Amen." I made this change in our family meal prayer twenty-five years ago. Now my grandchildren correct their Papa when he forgets and reverts back to the original form. This new way of praying before meals will help you focus on thanking the Lord for all our daily blessings.

OTHER READINGS: GENESIS 14:18–20; 1 CORINTHIANS 11:23–26

THIRTEENTH SUNDAY IN ORDINARY TIME

YES, BUT FIRST . . .

LUKE 9:51–62

[51] When the days for his being taken up were fulfilled, he resolutely determined to journey to Jerusalem, [52] and he sent messengers ahead of him. On the way they entered a Samaritan village to prepare for his reception there, [53] but they would not welcome him because the destination of his journey was Jerusalem. [54] When the disciples James and John saw this they asked, "Lord, do you want us to call down fire from heaven to consume them?" [55] Jesus turned and rebuked them, [56] and they journeyed to another village.

[57] As they were proceeding on their journey someone said to him, "I will follow you wherever you go." [58] Jesus answered him, "Foxes have dens and birds of the sky have nests, but the Son of Man has nowhere to rest his head." [59] And to another he said, "Follow me." But he replied, "[Lord,] let me go first and bury my father." [60] But he answered him, "Let the dead bury their dead. But you, go and proclaim the kingdom of God." [61] And another said, "I will follow you, Lord, but first let me say farewell to my family at home." [62] [To him] Jesus said, "No one who sets a hand to the plow and looks to what was left behind is fit for the kingdom of God."

The Gospel opens at a transition point. The public ministry in Galilee is complete. Jesus is moving on to Jerusalem where he and his disciples will celebrate Passover. He intends to take the shortest route, south through Samaria. By Jesus's day the animosity between the Jewish people in Galilee and Judea and those who lived in Samaria had been festering for centuries. Jesus has already passed safely through central Samaria before. In John 4, he encounters the woman at the well outside Shechem and is hosted by that village for three days. But Samaritans would only allow northbound Jews—heading away from the Jerusalem temple—to pass through their territory. Now an "advance team" of disciples returns with a report that Jesus and his southbound entourage are not welcome in the next village.

The brothers James and John are incensed. They ask if Jesus wants them to call down divine fire upon these inhospitable Samaritans. This call to incinerate a prospective enemy is reminiscent of the curse of the prophet Elijah when he was summoned to appear in the city of Samaria before King Ahaziah in 2 Kings 1:1–17. Jesus will have no part in such violence. He simply informs the group that they will take another route.

Now Jesus is passing through familiar territory and is recognized by people working in the nearby fields. Two of the men are intrigued and express a desire to join his discipleship group. A third is invited by Jesus to become a disciple. None of the three pass muster and Jesus moves along toward Jerusalem without them.

How does our knowledge of Middle Eastern culture inform this Gospel story? The first man Jesus passes by volunteers. He is willing to follow Jesus wherever he is going. Jesus responds: "Foxes have dens and birds of the sky have nests," but he has nowhere to rest his head. Jesus names himself "Son of Man," the messianic title from Daniel 7:14. "Foxes" and "birds" probably refer to King Herod, whom Jesus will call a "fox" (Luke 13:32), and the Romans, who march under the emblem of an eagle. Jesus is saying that following him as Messiah means rejecting the rule of both Herod and Rome. Jesus is a marked man who has opposed Herod in the past, and now he is heading to Jerusalem to lay down his life to these two worldly powers. Is this volunteer up to the challenge? Seemingly not.

Jesus invites the next person he meets to join the disciples, but he politely declines with a time-honored excuse: "Lord, let me go first and bury my father." His father is not dead. If he was, the son would not be working in the field. He would be at home mourning and preparing the body for burial. In essence he is saying that he wants to be allowed to support his father until he dies and is buried. He wants time and security. Then he would be willing to follow. Jesus is blunt: "Let the dead bury their dead." Or: I am more important than even your father. The people in the village will care for your aging parent. Jesus wants this man to come now. But he declines the invitation.

Now our third farmer addresses Jesus. He is plowing a field with a team of oxen. He asks for permission to follow Jesus—contingent on first returning to the village to say goodbye to his parents. This is a permission that he (and Jesus) know his father will never give. He is off the hook! Jesus reminds him that no one who puts his hand to the plow and looks back is fit for the kingdom of God. An ox driver has to be careful to plow in straight lines. You cannot look back at the work already done or you will plow over previously cut rows. That man had to be embarrassed—he had turned his head to speak to Jesus, and as he did his oxen had ruined work he had already finished. This man does not pass muster that day either.

The call and cost of discipleship is rising and will continue to rise the closer Jesus gets to his ultimate destination. Many are called but few are chosen. This seems to be the case this day.

—————————————— *Meditatio* ——————————————

Jesus rebukes James and John when they want to emulate Elijah, who called down fire from heaven to consume the soldiers sent to arrest him. Anger seems to have been a character flaw of that great prophet of Israel, who called down fire upon innocent messengers and also slaughtered the prophets of Baal rather than have them return to their villages bearing witness of God's mighty intercession on Elijah's behalf. Jesus is able to keep anger in check and find another way to his destination.

Jesus reveals what it means to be meek. We learn about meekness in the Sermon on the Mount when Jesus teaches that the meek are blessed and "shall inherit the earth." It is easy to confuse biblical meekness with cowardice or timidity in the face of a challenge. But the meekness Jesus demands of his disciples is best defined as "great strength under God's control." James and John start to learn this lesson in Jesus's response to their desire to destroy lives. When we read between the lines, Jesus is saying that no one should call down fire from heaven on these Samaritans, or on anyone else. When people do not cooperate, we are to place our strength under God's control and find another way to our destination.

Pray for this same gift of meekness in your walk with the Lord. Pray for the strength and courage to do great things for God and for the restraint needed to be named among the meek who will inherit the earth.

Oratio

In James 4:10 we learn what it means to be authentically humble (meek) in the presence of the Lord. This single verse is our prayer response to the Gospel. *"Humble yourself in the sight of the Lord, and he shall lift you up."*

Contemplatio

Do you remember making a "Yes, but first ..." response to the call of God in your life? If so you are in good company. Even Moses tried to excuse himself from God's call to be the liberator of his people (Exodus 3:11, 4:10). Gideon begged off his call to service in the presence of the angel of the Lord. He did not feel worthy of such a high calling (Judges 6:15). The prophets Jeremiah and Isaiah did not feel that they were the right men for the job. And don't get me started on the prophet Jonah!

We can be like the characters in this week's reading. We want to follow Jesus, but some of us are not quite ready. Others are unwilling to leave the comfort of the known to enter the wide world of discipleship. Jesus does not know where he is going to sleep that night, much less where he is going to find a meal. Thankfully, we know that God is patient. God keeps on calling. God is the proverbial "hound of heaven" who continually invites us into discipleship and service. God will keep calling. The next time God calls you, pause before you respond. Get beyond the "Yes, but first" and just say *yes*. Lord, you lead, and I will follow.

OTHER READINGS: 1 KINGS 19:16b, 19–21; GALATIANS 5.1, 13–18

PREPARE THE WAY

LUKE 10:1-12, 17-20

[1] After this the Lord appointed seventy[-two] others whom he sent ahead of him in pairs to every town and place he intended to visit. [2] He said to them, "The harvest is abundant but the laborers are few; so ask the master of the harvest to send out laborers for his harvest. [3] Go on your way; behold, I am sending you like lambs among wolves. [4] Carry no money bag, no sack, no sandals; and greet no one along the way. [5] Into whatever house you enter, first say, 'Peace to this household.' [6] If a peaceful person lives there, your peace will rest on him; but if not, it will return to you. [7] Stay in the same house and eat and drink what is offered to you, for the laborer deserves his payment. Do not move about from one house to another. [8] Whatever town you enter and they welcome you, eat what is set before you, [9] cure the sick in it and say to them, 'The kingdom of God is at hand for you.' [10] Whatever town you enter and they do not receive you, go out into the streets and say, [11] 'The dust of your town that clings to our feet, even that we shake off against you.' Yet know this: the kingdom of God is at hand. [12] I tell you, it will be more tolerable for Sodom on that day than for that town."

[17] The seventy[-two] returned rejoicing, and said, "Lord, even the demons are subject to us because of your name." [18] Jesus said, "I have observed Satan fall like lightning from the sky. [19] Behold, I have given you the power 'to tread upon serpents' and scorpions and upon the full force of the enemy and nothing will harm you. [20] Nevertheless, do not rejoice because the spirits are subject to you, but rejoice because your names are written in heaven."

───────────── *Lectio* ─────────────

Jesus and his disciples are on the move. Samaritan opposition has forced a change in travel plans. Jesus and the others will now have to travel down the Kings' Highway on the eastern side of the Jordan River to the ford-ing point near Jericho. They will travel through a well-watered agricul-tural region called Perea that was famous for its abundant yields of crops including olives and tomatoes.

Jesus sends out advance teams of two disciples each. They are charged to go ahead to the towns and villages along the route in anticipation of Jesus's eventual arrival. When they enter a village they are to heal those who are ill and preach the message about the kingdom of God. Jesus will follow and complete their work when he teaches the local villagers about what the kingdom of God will look like when it breaks forth in the world.

This ministry approach worked perfectly in Galilee. Healing activities will draw large crowds. The disciples are promised a new authority to cast out demons, which Jesus will refer to as the ability to "trample on snakes and scorpions." Satan will try to undermine their success (Luke 9:40) but they will overcome the enemy by powerful displays of healing author-ity. The crowds can then be influenced by the inspired preaching of the disciple-missionaries. When this work is completed they are to return to Jesus with a report about their efforts to seed the kingdom along the way.

Jesus warns the seventy-two that he is sending them out as lambs among wolves. What does he mean by this rather graphic and frighten-ing image? Wolves actually attack and eat lambs, after all. The lambs Jesus refers to are the individual members of his flock. Jesus is their shepherd. The animals in a flock belong to a single family. Jesus is sending these missionaries into foreign territory. No one has family here. They will be strangers among non-relatives. There will be danger involved. The local villagers may be aggressive. That is why they are to accept the first offer of hospitality when they come into a village.

Middle Eastern custom dictates that it will be the elders in the village who will welcome them. Their hospitality will provide protection from any potential aggressors (see Genesis 19:1–2). Accept this offer and pray the *shalom* of God upon their home. Don't move from house to house. This is a temporary assignment. Some villages will welcome you, others will not. Jesus directs the missionaries to make a public spectacle of those who reject their work of healing and preaching. Taking off your sandals and slapping them together is a visual way of saying that you don't want to take the dirt from their street with you when you leave!

Jesus also tells them not to greet anyone on the road. That seems a bit harsh until you understand how Middle Easterners greet one another. This sort of greeting is formal and time consuming. It involves the recounting of family histories, the relative health and well-being of each member of each extended family, and their present-day engagements. This is the kind of greeting that Mary shared with Elizabeth when she arrived unexpectedly in the village pregnant with the Messiah. These greetings can take up to thirty minutes. Jesus warns the missionaries that if you stop to greet everyone you meet on the way you will never make it to the next village!

The seventy-two have their commission and are sent off into uncharted territory to prepare the way for the Lord.

Meditatio

"Into whatever house you enter, first say, 'Peace to this household.'" The English *peace* is translating a Hebrew concept, *shalom.* Our Western understanding of peace is different from the intention of Jesus and his missionary team. In the West peace is typically defined as the absence of trouble or conflict. Shalom has a far deeper meaning. On a basic level, *shalom* used in context can mean simply "hello" or "goodbye." But the concept also conveys the hope of a blessing from God that will result in a sense of wellness and wholeness upon the home and its occupants. It is a prayer that everyone and everything in the home be whole, complete, perfect, and full. Jesus reminds them that if their shalom is not received it can be taken back.

Shalom is God's vision for the emphatic goodness of all relationships. It is unrelated to circumstances. Paul and his ministry partner Silas knew this kind of God-gifted peace in Acts when they were in prison after having been publicly flogged. Even then they were "praying and singing hymns to God" as the other prisoners in the jail listened (Acts 16:22–25). Paul and Silas knew the true shalom of God. Keep this in mind the next time you visit a friend. Wish them *shalom* with this intention of wholeness and wellness in mind.

I am reminded of the call of a great missionary, the prophet Isaiah. In his vision recorded in Isaiah 6 the prophet hears a voice asking, "Whom shall I send? Who will go for us?" The response of the prophet will be our prayer response this week: "Here I am, send me!"

Contemplatio

Reserve a few moments this week to pray for missionaries. Every faith community can support the work of those who are sent out to heal, preach, and teach in the name of Jesus. In some communities the missionaries are actual members of the congregation. My uncle David's Trinity Baptist Church has a wonderful missionary map. Brightly colored stick pins are inserted in the various countries where members of his congregation are serving. Each time you pass by the board you are encouraged to pause and pray for their safety and success in proclaiming the gospel of the kingdom.

In the Catholic world most missionaries are vowed religious men and women who serve the Lord in every far-flung location on the planet. When I pray for missionaries I am praying for those countless men and women who have dedicated their lives to the work of spreading the net of salvation deeper and wider than I could ever imagine.

So pray for the missionaries serving the Lord as members of your communities. Support their missions as you are inspired and able. It is one way we can participate in the spreading of the gospel to the ends of the earth.

OTHER READINGS: ISAIAH 66:10–14c; GALATIANS 6:14–18

FIFTEENTH SUNDAY IN ORDINARY TIME

MY NEIGHBOR

LUKE 10:25-37

[25] There was a scholar of the law who stood up to test him and said, "Teacher, what must I do to inherit eternal life?" [26] Jesus said to him, "What is written in the law? How do you read it?" [27] He said in reply,

"You shall love the Lord, your God, with all your heart, with all your being, with all your strength, and with all your mind, and your neighbor as yourself." [28] He replied to him, "You have answered correctly; do this and you will live."

[29] But because he wished to justify himself, he said to Jesus, "And who is my neighbor?" [30] Jesus replied, "A man fell victim to robbers as he went down from Jerusalem to Jericho. They stripped and beat him and went off leaving him half-dead. [31] A priest happened to be going down that road, but when he saw him, he passed by on the opposite side. [32] Likewise a Levite came to the place, and when he saw him, he passed by on the opposite side. [33] But a Samaritan traveler who came upon him was moved with compassion at the sight. [34] He approached the victim, poured oil and wine over his wounds and bandaged them. Then he lifted him up on his own animal, took him to an inn and cared for him. [35] The next day he took out two silver coins and gave them to the innkeeper with the instruction, 'Take care of him. If you spend more than what I have given you, I shall repay you on my way back.' [36] Which of these three, in your opinion, was neighbor to the robbers' victim?" [37] He answered, "The one who treated him with mercy." Jesus said to him, "Go and do likewise."

—— *Lectio* ——

Our Gospel opens as disciples gather around Jesus to listen to him teach. Jesus is seated next to a "scholar of the law," an expert in the law of God. As seated figures they are equals and would be surrounded by standing students. This scholar stands to ask Jesus a question, thus assuming the position of a student. A public inquiry of this kind would be perceived as a threat. Is he trying to trip up Jesus? This explains why Jesus responds with a question of his own, revealing his own genius as a scholar.

The man asks, "What must I do to inherit eternal life?" Jesus responds with his own question. "What is written in the law? How do you read [or interpret] it?" The scholar replies with a summary of the law that mirrors Jesus's own response (see Matthew 22:37–40), and Jesus tells him, "You have answered correctly; do this and you will live." But the exchange is not

Be Vigilant! Lectio Divina for Year C

over. The scholar poses a follow-up to try to reclaim his own honor. "And who is my neighbor?" Jesus now sets up his next question to the scholar with a parable—the famous parable of the Good Samaritan.

The parables of Jesus are stories, not references to events ripped from the local headlines. Each is intended to reveal a surprise element that leaves the listener in doubt as to its precise meaning. The parables are open ended, with the application of the teaching left to the listener. Our parable opens with the introduction of some stock characters from Jewish storytelling. These stories usually involve a priest, a Levite, and then a Jewish layperson who will swoop in and save the day.

The parable opens ominously. A man traveling from Jerusalem to Jericho is waylaid by robbers, beaten, and left half-dead on the roadside. He is naked and unconscious. The scene is set for the failure of the priest, and the listening audience is not disappointed. A priest appears in the story, sees the man, and passes by on the opposite side. In the Torah a primary means of ritual defilement is contact with a dead body, and in the Jewish oral law this was expanded for priests to include defilement by any contact with a non-Jew. This priest could not be too careful! He did not want to risk potential defilement, which would require an expensive journey back to Jerusalem and a two-week delay of his return to his home village.

The next person to appear in the story is a Levite, a member of a priestly family. He follows the example of the first character. If he stops to assist the wounded fellow, he would be criticizing the priest's interpretation of the law. He too passes by on the other side of the road. Finally, the expected hero of the story appears: the pious and caring Jewish layperson. This is where Jesus shocks the audience. The Jewish layperson is replaced by a Samaritan. Samaritans were viewed as renegade Jews who denied the legitimacy of the Jerusalem temple. They had shared mutual animosity with the Jews of Judea and Galilee for over 700 years! Recall that in Luke 9:52–56 James and John want to "call down fire from heaven" to consume a Samaritan village. The audience would expect a Samaritan in the story to finish off the wounded man. Instead he offers aid and assistance.

The Samaritan proves to be "neighbor" to this unidentifiable victim. Samaritans and Jews came from the same religious stock and shared the same Torah. Each had to answer the question, "who is my neighbor?" Is my neighbor only my fellow Israelite or fellow Samaritan, or does the commandment extend to heretics, or even Gentiles? The Samaritan in the parable acts as an agent of God. He arrives on the scene and immediately feels compassion for the wounded fellow. In a manner similar to God in Hosea 6:1, he binds up the wounds using wine and oil for medicine. Then he transports the man to an inn in Jericho where he can provide additional care and makes provision for future treatments that he pays for in advance. He promises the innkeeper that he will return and will then cover any other debts that his "neighbor" may incur.

When the parable ends Jesus asks the scholar of the law which of the three characters in the story proved to be a neighbor to the victim. The scholar responds correctly. It is the character who treated him with mercy, with tenderness and care. "Go and do likewise" is his final counsel.

Meditatio

"And who is my neighbor" is a question that continues to require interpretation by students of the law. Is your neighbor only someone like you, or is there a broader interpretation that calls for acts of love and service to be extended to everyone in need you encounter? Jesus points us toward the latter interpretation. Your neighbor is not just your fellow Israelite but can also be a hated enemy. The Samaritan character upsets expectations and challenges those who hear to reconsider their long-held assumptions.

How do you respond to the question? Who is your neighbor? What boundaries have you placed on the category of neighbor in your life? What would it take to break those boundaries down? What kind of service opportunities would work best toward this goal?

Oratio

The Prayer of St. Francis will serve us well as a response to the Gospel this week.

Make me a channel of your peace
Where there is hatred let me bring love
Where there is injury, your pardon, Lord
And where there's doubt, true faith in you.

"Go and do likewise." Jesus directs the scholar of the law to go and act. He shouldn't wait, ponder, and pause before taking action to assist another. In Jewish theology deeds always trump creeds. What you say you believe must come out in the way you live. The evidence of your faith is your actions; the way you live your life is your witness of God to the world.

Jesus uses this parable to teach the disciples to follow the example of the hated Samaritan who feels compassion for the injured person. What the robbers did to the man, this seeming enemy undoes by his willingness to go the extra mile in service. That will be our challenge this week. Pray for the opportunity to go the extra mile in service to an unexpected recipient. Follow the example of the Samaritan and "go and do likewise."

OTHER READINGS: DEUTERONOMY 30:10–14; COLOSSIANS 1:15–20

SIXTEENTH SUNDAY IN ORDINARY TIME

A MARY HEART IN A MARTHA WORLD

LUKE 10:38–42

[38] As they continued their journey he entered a village where a woman whose name was Martha welcomed him. [39] She had a sister named Mary [who] sat beside the Lord at his feet listening to him speak. [40] Martha, burdened with much serving, came to him and said, "Lord, do you not care that my sister has left me by myself to do the serving? Tell her to help me." [41] The Lord said to her in reply, "Martha, Martha, you are anxious and worried about many things. [42] There is need of only one thing. Mary has chosen the better part and it will not be taken from her."

—— *Lectio* ——

While the chronology of this Gospel story is difficult to pin down the geography is not. Jesus and the disciples are on their way to Jerusalem to celebrate Passover. The group arrives in the village of Bethany where Jesus is greeted by his good friend Martha. Martha and her two siblings, Mary and Lazarus, share a home in the village and would have been delighted that their friend and teacher Jesus has come to visit. Martha welcomes Jesus into her home. As a responsible Middle Eastern host Martha (and presumably her sister Mary) would be pressed immediately into service, procuring, preparing, and then providing food and drink for their guests.

It is the custom in the Middle East that the women of the household prepare and serve the food to the men. Meals are served and eaten in gender-specific groups. Only children under twelve can move freely between these separate meals. These cultural expectations open additional insight on the position of Mary, whom we meet seated at the feet of Jesus. She has assumed the position of a student to Jesus. This would have been a surprise to those present in the room that day.

Luke notes the many times Jesus honors women as part of the growing group of his disciples. In Luke 8:3 he reminds the reader that many women were helping to support the work of Jesus out of their own means. Now we get to know Martha a bit better. We learn that she is "burdened with much serving." There are unexpected guests in her home and Martha is culturally conditioned to serve them a meal. She wonders why Jesus, a man of her time who shares her cultural understanding of household roles, allows Mary to remain in the role of student (seated at the teacher's feet) while she struggles to produce the meal by herself. And what about her sister? Why won't she help? Martha is rightfully upset. She approaches Jesus to demand him to tell her sister to help, for goodness sake!

Jesus replies to Martha in a manner that suggests the bond of friendship they share. "Martha, Martha." He speaks her name twice. These two know each other well. Jesus knows that Mary should assist her sister, but he will not deny her the opportunity to continue to be formed as a disciple by his teaching. Jesus acknowledges that Martha is "anxious and worried" about many things. Jesus certainly appreciates what it takes to provide for so many. But Jesus assures Martha that only one thing is needed. He looks at Mary, seated at his feet. She is a student and he is her teacher. Mary has chosen what is better. She wants to listen and learn. Martha will have to make do with the help at hand because Mary is going to stay right where she is.

Mary has chosen the better way. She is seated at the feet of Jesus. She is an engaged disciple, ready to listen and learn from her rabbi. Mary wants to be a disciple. Jesus honors her desire. It will not be taken from her.

The holiest people I know are women. My grandmother, my mother, my aunts, and other women of faith have all had a positive influence on my walk with the Lord. This would not be typical in the time of Jesus. In New Testament times women were expected to perform specific cultural roles. Works of household service, becoming a marriage partner, bearing and raising children. The list goes on and on but would not necessarily include being formed as a disciple.

Jesus broke through those cultural barriers with his students. Jesus taught both men and women about the meaning of the kingdom of God. He commissioned both men and women to take the message of salvation to the ends of the earth. Women and men are of equal value in God's eyes and both are valued in Jesus's ministry. Women in his company, like Mary (and others) had chosen this better way, and they were not denied.

The various roles women played in the ministry of Jesus did not align with the cultural expectations of women in the Middle East. Mary is a wonderful example for our meditation this week. She took a place at the feet of Jesus. She wanted to learn directly from her rabbi. Additional hospitality concerns would be covered by others while Mary continued to listen to the Lord. Do we follow her example? Do we strive to choose the better way? Are we committed to an ongoing study of the Word? How will you find your seat at the feet of Jesus this week?

Oratio

This prayer is adapted from The Gospel Coalition. We live in a "Martha" world of many distractions, never-ending demands, and over-stimulation. This prayer will help ease our anxiety and worry.

Lord Jesus, help me cultivate a Mary heart in a Martha world. My problem isn't the world I inhabit, but the heart that inhabits me. You are the "one thing worth being concerned about"; you are the "one thing" that will never be taken from me. Amen.

What could be our action response this week? One consideration would be to identify yourself in one of the two sisters in the Gospel story. Are you a Martha? Ready and able to receive guests, purchase food, and provide hospitality? Is that your gift of service to the community? If so, be diligent in sharing this gift. Are you a Mary? Do you prefer to sit at the feet of the Lord and learn from him? To spend time in the Word, getting to know Jesus better? If so, remember that you are being trained up so that you can share your gift with others too. The "Marthas" in the church and their lives of active service are meant to complement and balance the contemplative and studious life of the "Marys" in the community. So who do you identify with this week? What should you learn from the other kind of person? Are you a Martha or a Mary? How does that identification challenge you in the way you will live your faith this week?

OTHER READINGS: GENESIS 18:1–10a; COLOSSIANS 1:24–28

SEVENTEENTH SUNDAY IN ORDINARY TIME

KEEP ON ASKING, SEEKING, AND KNOCKING

LUKE 11:1-13

[1] He was praying in a certain place, and when he had finished, one of his disciples said to him, "Lord, teach us to pray just as John taught his disciples." [2] He said to them, "When you pray, say:

Father, hallowed be your name,
your kingdom come.
[3] Give us each day our daily bread
[4] and forgive us our sins
for we ourselves forgive everyone in debt to us,
and do not subject us to the final test."

[5] And he said to them, "Suppose one of you has a friend to whom he goes at midnight and says, 'Friend, lend me three loaves of bread, [6] for

a friend of mine has arrived at my house from a journey and I have nothing to offer him,' [7] and he says in reply from within, 'Do not bother me; the door has already been locked and my children and I are already in bed. I cannot get up to give you anything.' [8] I tell you, if he does not get up to give him the loaves because of their friendship, he will get up to give him whatever he needs because of his persistence.

[9] "And I tell you, ask and you will receive; seek and you will find; knock and the door will be opened to you. [10] For everyone who asks, receives; and the one who seeks, finds; and to the one who knocks, the door will be opened. [11] What father among you would hand his son a snake when he asks for a fish? [12] Or hand him a scorpion when he asks for an egg? [13] If you then, who are wicked, know how to give good gifts to your children, how much more will the Father in heaven give the holy Spirit to those who ask him?"

--- *Lectio* ---

This week Jesus teaches his disciples about prayer in three separate stories that Luke has grouped by theme. The Gospel opens with the disciples asking Jesus to "teach" them to pray. They remind Jesus that John the Baptist taught his disciples how they should pray. The prayer format Jesus teaches them is now called the "Our Father" and is familiar to all Christians. This prayer is simple and direct and focused on the needs of the community of faith. Jesus counsels us to petition God as our Father for "our" daily bread, that God forgive "our" sins, and that God lead "us" away from temptation. Do you hear the communal language? This prayer is meant to unite us to one another and to God.

The second teaching on prayer involves a parable. The parables of Jesus always contain a shocking element that arrests the listener and draws our attention to the rest of the parable, which ends abruptly and without an obvious application. The work of insight and application is left to the hearers. In this story one friend comes to another friend in the middle of the night. He needs help with an obligation of hospitality. A guest has arrived unannounced and his host must secure all that is needed to provide a proper meal. We assume that the host in the parable has nothing to set before the unexpected visitor. In the Middle East the host will move throughout the village to seek from friends and neighbors what is needed for his guest. The request may be as simple as bread. The host would be looking for fresh, whole loaves to present at table. The honor of the village is at stake. Will the villagers respond favorably or not?

The shock element of this parable is that the friend, awakened behind closed doors, refuses to open up and provide. His excuses are comical. The door is locked and his children are asleep. We know that a door can easily be unlocked and that children typically sleep through anything. His friend rejects his request and is not willing to assist in meeting the demands of village hospitality to strangers. This is a cardinal sin in the Middle East, where a guest would be greeted with words similar to, "My village and I are honored by your presence."

By the end of the parable the request, although originally denied, will be honored. The cultural pressure is monumental. The man will get up, unlock the door, wake the children, and be willing to "give him as much as he needs." The man inside knows that his friend will be going from house to house. From one home he will find bread, from another vegetables, from a third drink. If this fellow does not open and provide his part as requested, he will be shamed in the morning by everyone else in the village.

Now Jesus addresses the issue of persistence in prayer. He teaches his disciples that when they pray, they need to be willing to ask, to seek, and to knock. These words in the original Greek of the New Testament use the infinitive tense (think of the word infinity). Properly translated you would add an "-ing" ending to each word. Ask and keep on asking. Seek and keep on seeking. Knock and keep on knocking and you will find your answer in time. Jesus contrasts the wisdom of human fathers with the wisdom of God. Human fathers know the difference between a snake (a freshwater eel in the Sea of Galilee) and a fish. One is not kosher and the other is. Fathers know the difference between a balled-up scorpion that resembles a wild bird's egg and the actual egg itself. One is dangerous and the other is a delicacy. God as our Father knows this too and will always give good gifts to those who ask (pray) with persistence.

In New Testament times Jewish prayers were long and formulaic. Prayer was a public event performed on street corners so that men could be seen (Matthew 6:5). Jesus doesn't want his disciples to pray like this. He also counsels against praying like "babbling" pagans who believed they would be heard because of the multiplication of many words (Matthew 6:7). The prayer style of pagans was contractual and precise. Pagan gods were capricious, always ready to trip up the petitioner. One had to be specific with any petition to these gods. The gifted touch of King Midas could turn a stone to gold—but also a child. One could never be too careful.

Jesus teaches his disciples to pray in a simple, concise, and clear manner. Our prayer should be focused not just on ourselves but on the needs of the community. In *Prayer, Our Deepest Longing,* Fr. Ronald Rolheiser notes that the disciples wanted Jesus to teach them to pray like he did because they wanted access to Jesus's power to "be big-hearted, to love beyond his own tribe, to love the poor and the rich alike, to live inside charity, joy, peace, patience, goodness, long-suffering, fidelity, mildness, and chastity, despite everything within life that militates against these virtues."

Our prayer response this week will be a thoughtful and private recitation of the "Our Father." Carve out a few extra moments in your quiet time each day this week to pray it slowly and thoughtfully, paying special attention to the communal aspect of the prayer.

How do you pray best? Where do you pray best? When do you pray best? These are important questions to ask yourself as we engage Jesus and his teaching about prayer. I am reminded of an insight I gleaned from a rabbi at the Hebrew University in Jerusalem who taught Christian students about Jewish faith practices. In one seminar I was introduced to the Jewish prayer practice called "shuckling." When Orthodox Jewish persons pray, they typically engage as many of their senses as possible. They hold the word in the form of a book. They see the words with their eyes. They whisper the words with their mouths so that these words can be heard by their ears. This is done while they stand and sway as they read and pray. The intent is to engage every joint and sinew in the practice of prayer, to use every possible sense so they will not lose focus and become distracted.

Christians may find this prayer style disconcerting. How can anyone focus with so much activity going on all around? Jewish people wonder how Christians can remain attentive to prayers that can be formal, patterned, and passive. Try a new style of prayer this week. Stand to pray. Read the Bible text aloud. Walk and pray. See if any of these sorts of practices enhance your prayer experience this week.

OTHER READINGS: GENESIS 18:20–32; COLOSSIANS 2:12-14

EIGHTEENTH SUNDAY IN ORDINARY TIME

RICH IN WHAT MATTERS TO GOD

LUKE 12:13-21

[13] Someone in the crowd said to him, "Teacher, tell my brother to share the inheritance with me." [14] He replied to him, "Friend, who appointed me as your judge and arbitrator?" [15] Then he said to the crowd, "Take care to guard against all greed, for though one may be rich, one's life does not consist of possessions."

[16] Then he told them a parable. "There was a rich man whose land produced a bountiful harvest. [17] He asked himself, 'What shall I do, for I do not have space to store my harvest?' [18] And he said, 'This is what I shall do: I shall tear down my barns and build larger ones. There I shall store all my grain and other goods [19] and I shall say to myself, "Now as for you, you have so many good things stored up for many years, rest, eat, drink, be merry!"' [20] But God said to him, 'You fool, this night your life will be demanded of you; and the things you have prepared, to whom will they belong?' [21] Thus will it be for the one who stores up treasure for himself but is not rich in what matters to God."

The scene is set. The Gospel opens as a brother engages Jesus as a judge, seeking a decision that will give him an advantage over his older sibling in a property dispute. Customs in the Middle East dictate that the eldest son always inherits twice as much as any other sibling. With two brothers in this Gospel scenario, the elder would receive two thirds of the land and the younger the remaining third. The younger brother is not pleased with this arrangement and wants Jesus to advocate on his behalf. His intent is to use Jesus to get what he wants from his sibling.

Jesus sees through this ruse to the heart of the matter. He will not judge between them, but his reply renders an assessment of the motivations of this younger brother. Jesus warns the young man to guard against all greed and reminds him that a person's life—our basic existence—does not consist in acquisition. By now a large crowd has gathered. Jesus seizes this opportunity to teach them all by telling them a parable.

Our parable involves a single character. This "rich man" is a landowner who has never worked in an actual field. He has rented his land out to tenants. Through their efforts and the grace of God an agricultural windfall has come his way. How will he respond?

Jesus makes his point clear as "rich man" begins a series of deliberations—with himself! Has he no confidants? A decision to tear down and build larger barns would typically involve long drawn-out conversations with civic leaders at the city gate. Compare this with some other parables of Jesus—the shepherd who finds his lost sheep rejoices with others in the village; the woman who finds her lost coin shares the good news with all her female friends. The rich man in our parable speaks with no one except himself. He comes to the conclusion that with so many things stored away he will have no worries. He can eat, drink, and be merry! It sounds like a great plan, but he is "gravely" mistaken.

The rich man already has everything he needs to live a life of ease. His intention to build larger barns is blatantly selfish. He wants to store the grain so that he can eventually sell it back to the tenants. He would keep it for himself and not share his good fortune. He hatches his plan without consulting with anyone except himself. The parable ends abruptly as God demands his life. He will be judged harshly because he is not "rich" in what matters to God. And what is it that matters to God? That is the subject of this week's Meditatio.

Meditatio

The rich man in the parable missed an important cultural opportunity. The sudden wealth acquired from a bountiful harvest came with a price. The economic system in the time of Jesus was one of limited goods. He was certainly aware of the cultural expectation to share his bounty with others in the village. But it appears he was not concerned about the public and religious consequences of his decision. Family, friends, and neighbors would have counseled him to abandon the decision to build bigger storage barns and act instead like a Middle Eastern patron and share his abundant harvest with those in need. In doing this his honor would rise, for everyone in the village would be compelled to speak well of him. This is how he could have been "rich in what matters to God." The blessings bestowed on him by God were meant to be shared with others. He already has all that he needed to live free from care. Now, in a position to help the less fortunate, he chooses not to—a choice with eternal ramifications.

How will we become "rich in what matters to God"? The answer involves an awareness and appreciation of our place in community. The blessings God sends *are* meant for us, but are also meant to be passed on to bless others. Widows, orphans, the poor and infirm, the elderly and the weak—the vulnerable are always on the mind of God, who blesses us so that we can bless them with our time, our talents, and our treasure.

Oratio

The Gospel opens with brothers engaged in a public dispute about an inheritance. We will draw upon Psalm 133 as our prayer response to the Gospel this week. "How good and pleasant it is, when brothers dwell together as one! Like fine oil on the head, running down on the beard, upon the beard of Aaron, upon the collar of his robe. Like dew of Hermon coming down upon the mountains of Zion. There the LORD has decreed a blessing, life for evermore!"

"Sleep is sweet to the laborer, whether there is little or much to eat; but the abundance of the rich allows them no sleep" (Ecclesiastes 5:11). This saying from the wisdom of Ecclesiastes informs our contemplation this week. A rich person can't sleep because he must constantly guard the abundance that has come his way. The rich man in the parable would build bigger barns in his effort to safeguard his agricultural windfall. The workers sleep soundly. They have completed the heavy work in the field and know that all growth and agricultural bounty comes directly from God. They have a hand in the work of God; not so the rich man.

St. Ambrose once preached a sermon on this parable and suggested that the rich man did not need to build bigger barns to store his grain. The saint suggested that there would have been ample room to store the grain in the mouths of the poor. Very true indeed.

What is our response going to be to the Gospel this week? I support two charities that feed the hungry around the world. My wife and I make a monthly donation to each so that from our bounty we can share with others less fortunate than ourselves. You can do some research and find a way you too can support those who don't have enough. In this way we can all become "rich in what matters to God."

OTHER READINGS: ECCLESIASTES 1:2; 2:21–23; COLOSSIANS 3:1–5, 9–11

NINETEENTH SUNDAY IN ORDINARY TIME

INEXHAUSTIBLE TREASURE

LUKE 12:32–48

³² Do not be afraid any longer, little flock, for your Father is pleased to give you the kingdom. ³³ Sell your belongings and give alms. Provide money bags for yourselves that do not wear out, an inexhaustible treasure in heaven that no thief can reach nor moth destroy. ³⁴ For where your treasure is, there also will your heart be.

³⁵ "Gird your loins and light your lamps ³⁶ and be like servants who await their master's return from a wedding, ready to open immediately when he comes and knocks. ³⁷ Blessed are those servants whom the master finds vigilant on his arrival. Amen, I say to you, he will gird himself, have them recline at table, and proceed to wait on them. ³⁸ And should he come in the second or third watch and find them prepared in this way, blessed are those servants. ³⁹ Be sure of this: if the master of the house had known the hour when the thief was coming, he would not have let his house be broken into. ⁴⁰ You also must be prepared, for at an hour you do not expect, the Son of Man will come."

⁴¹ Then Peter said, "Lord, is this parable meant for us or for everyone?" ⁴² And the Lord replied, "Who, then, is the faithful and prudent steward whom the master will put in charge of his servants to distribute [the] food allowance at the proper time? ⁴³ Blessed is that servant whom his master on arrival finds doing so. ⁴⁴ Truly, I say to you, he will put him in charge of all his property. ⁴⁵ But if that servant says to himself, 'My master is delayed in coming,' and begins to beat the menservants and the maidservants, to eat and drink and get drunk, ⁴⁶ then that servant's master will come on an unexpected day and at an unknown hour and will punish him severely and assign him a place with the unfaithful. ⁴⁷ That servant who knew his master's will but did not make preparations nor act in accord with his will shall be beaten severely; ⁴⁸ and the servant who was ignorant of his master's will but acted in a way deserving of a severe beating shall be beaten only lightly. Much will be required of the person entrusted with much, and still more will be demanded of the person entrusted with more."

Lectio

Jesus has been teaching his disciples that they need to live lives completely dependent upon God. He has reminded them that since even the smallest things are beyond their control, they should not be anxious about anything. Their Father knows what they need. His disciples are to seek his kingdom and all these other things will also be given to them. This is where the Gospel reading begins. Jesus tells his "little flock" not to be anxious. He promises them that God is pleased to give them "the kingdom." What kind of kingdom did Jesus have in mind? And who makes up the "little flock"? We will address both of these questions this week.

Luke wants us to know that the "little flock" is a reference to Jesus's closest associates. Jesus encourages the twelve disciples to sell their belongings and use the proceeds to provide alms to the poor. In this way they will acquire a money bag that will not wear out, one that is eternal and filled with the blessings of God, who will reward them for their generosity to others. That treasure will be on deposit in heaven where no thief or moth can destroy it. Jesus reminds the twelve that their hearts will be where their treasure is. The biblical "heart" is equivalent to the Western "mind." If your treasure is in heaven, your heart is in heaven and your thoughts will be of heaven. This is the mindset Jesus demands of those who will serve others as leaders in the new community of faith, the church.

The twelve are now presented with a parable that challenges their understanding of leadership and service. Jesus begins with a common image, a wedding. The wedding day has arrived and the groom leaves his father's house to collect his bride in another part of the region. No one knows how long he will be gone but they are certain of one thing: the groom will return ready to celebrate. It is the responsibility of the household servants to greet him when his arrival is announced. They are to be vigilant and ready to spring into service at a moment's notice.

Then Jesus delivers a surprise. In the parable this groom arrives and shocks everyone as he girds himself and invites *them* to recline at table. The groom serves the servants at his own wedding feast! How can this be? Jesus will demonstrate this kind of leadership at the Last Supper when he will rise from the Passover table, gird his loins, and wash the feet of each apostle. Then Peter will try to refuse the act of service. Now it is Peter, leader of the twelve, who asks Jesus about the intent of his teaching. "Lord, is this parable meant for us or for everyone?" The coded answer is that the parable is meant for them, the twelve. They are expected to remain vigilant and ready to serve until Jesus the groom returns, unannounced and at a time they least expect. It will go well with them if he finds them serving dutifully and not abusing anyone in the household while he is away. If they pass the test, they will be put in charge of all his property and receive the honor associated with that position. If they fail, they will be punished most severely. To those to whom much is given much is required.

<hr>

Meditatio

Past, present, future. As Western-educated men and women we typically find ourselves fixated on the future. Our hope is in a better future for our children, our church, and our world. The lessons of the past pale before the excitement of what may be just around the corner!

This was not true for our Middle Eastern ancestors of faith. Common people in the biblical era lived and found meaning in an "extended" present tense. There was too much to do now to waste time wondering about what the future might hold. And what of the elites, the religious leaders? They looked to the past, to the ancient traditions of the community. It was their responsibility to interpret these past teachings so that they could be followed in the present. Yet in our Gospel reading Jesus speaks in clear terms about the future. I find this very interesting.

Jesus began this teaching warning about the pitfalls of anxiety. You can do nothing to affect the future. His followers should wait with patient expectation for the arrival of the Son of Man while at the same time paying attention to the demands of the present. It remains good advice today. Which of us can add a day to our lives through worry or anxiety? We need to learn this lesson again and again. To honor the lessons of the past. To live in the present moment. And to hold a secure hope in the promise of the return of our Messiah in the future.

<hr>

Oratio

Lord, help me develop the heart of a faithful servant. A heart that will be ready to assist others, to give alms generously, and to share my many blessings with those in need. Create in me that clean heart and renew in me a steadfast spirit.

<hr>

Contemplatio

Jesus directs the apostles to sell their possessions, rely upon God, and give alms. In Jesus's day almsgiving was a duty for the person of faith. The

Torah teaches that you are to pray (twice daily), fast (annually on Yom Kippur), and give alms (all the time). Almsgiving differs from simply giving someone money. An almsworthy recipient has a recognizable physical challenge that your generosity can help alleviate. In the Middle East a person who receives alms responds by saying, "you're welcome." That seems odd, but your fulfilling your duty to give alms was possible because God put that particular almsworthy person in front of you that day. That person has assisted you in accomplishing your religious duty.

How do we find almsworthy persons today? I trust my local bishop and the outreach he champions through our annual appeal to find and assist the truly almsworthy in the diocese of Phoenix. You might want to consider making a contribution to a similar outreach in your community this week as a faith response to the Gospel.

OTHER READINGS: WISDOM 18:6-9; HEBREWS 11:1-2, 8-19

TWENTIETH SUNDAY IN ORDINARY TIME

TO SET THE EARTH ON FIRE

LUKE 12:49-53

⁴⁹ "I have come to set the earth on fire, and how I wish it were already blazing! ⁵⁰ There is a baptism with which I must be baptized, and how great is my anguish until it is accomplished! ⁵¹ Do you think that I have come to establish peace on the earth? No, I tell you, but rather division. ⁵² From now on a household of five will be divided, three against two and two against three; ⁵³ a father will be divided against his son and a son against his father, a mother against her daughter and a daughter against her mother, a mother-in-law against her daughter-in-law and a daughter-in-law against her mother-in-law."

Lectio

"I have come to set the earth on fire, and how I wish it were already blazing!" These words of Jesus shock us, as well they should. What is he referring to?

This week I am beholden to the scholar John J. Pilch. His groundbreaking work on Jesus and the New Testament period sheds fresh light on texts like this that are otherwise difficult to understand.

In Jesus's day each family built and maintained an earthenware oven in the shape of a half dome. A heat source was kindled inside, and flatbreads were baked on its outer surface. Curiously, the fuel for these earthen ovens was a clever mixture of camel dung and salt, formed into pods or patties and dried in the sun. These early "fuel cells" used salt from the Dead Sea, which contains significant traces of magnesium. This element burns at a high temperature and makes possible the efficient combustion of the dried camel dung. The fuel was placed in the earthen ovens on blocks of salt. Once the fuel pod was lit, the person tending the oven would occasionally toss more salt on it to make it burn hotter. This common oven is what Jesus is referring to when we read that he has come to "set the earth on fire." Jesus has come to turn up the heat.

These "earthen oven" insights also help us understand some related sayings of Jesus. In Luke 14:34–35, Jesus teaches that when salt loses its "taste"—its catalytic capacity—it is "fit neither for the soil nor for the manure pile; it is thrown out." Eventually the salt's ability to increase the heat is used up and it needs to be replaced. And when Jesus in Matthew 5:13 challenges his disciples to be the "salt of the earth" he means that if they are going to follow him they also have to be willing to be used by God until they are spent, like the fuel source of these earthen ovens.

After this initial statement Jesus turns his attention to the baptism he must endure. This is a reference to his death. He speaks of the anguish he will go through until it is accomplished. The heat has been turned up, the oven is blazing! The time for the work he must accomplish on this side of the grave has begun. Jesus wonders why his disciples ever thought he intended to bring peace on the earth (remember the insights of the earthen oven). He does not promise them peace but, shockingly, division.

———————————— *Meditatio* ————————————

Let's take a moment to consider the nature of salt. In Matthew 5:13 Jesus teaches his disciples that if they are going to follow him, they will need to be "salt" for the earth. Many have wondered what this image means. Salt was indeed used to preserve fish in Jesus's day, but salt as a flavor-enhancing condiment was rarely used in that desert climate.

Do you suppose that we are to carefully preserve ancient teachings and traditions? To "salt" them away for later use? Does Jesus intend us to be agents of flavoring, to make the world taste better for our presence? I think not. But salt in a wound burns. It feels like the wound is on fire. Now we are getting somewhere!

The salt in the camel dung fuel cells and the loose salt added to the fire was a catalytic agent that increased the temperature of the earthen oven. This is what Jesus had in mind. We are to be *that* kind of salt of the earth. If we are to follow Jesus, we have to be willing to be used by the Lord to make a small flame burn brighter and hotter; and this until we are spent and are no longer salty.

That is a challenge worth our meditation. Are we willing to be the salt that Jesus will use to kindle the fire of faith to a new intensity? Am I willing to be spent in this way? What will I be risking and for how long? How difficult will it be? Reflect also that fire in the biblical world often refers to purification. These considerations can fuel our meditation as we prepare for church this weekend.

────────────────── *Oratio* ──────────────────

We will lean into a prophecy of Micah this week as our prayer response to the Gospel. The prophet knows that an enemy nation is planning an attack, but he decides to stand strong in the midst of fear. This prayer for protection, paraphrased from Micah 7:14–15, will be ours this week. "Oh God, shepherd us with your staff. We are the flock of your heritage. Restore to us lives in the woodland and in the midst of an orchard. Let us feed again in Bashan and Gilead as in the days of old; as in the days when you came from the land of Egypt and showed us wonderful signs."

────────────────── *Contemplatio* ──────────────────

"It only takes a spark to get the fire going, and soon all those around can warm up to its glowing. That's how it is with God's love. Once you've experienced it, you spread his love to everyone. You want to pass it on."

These words are from a 1969 song called "Pass It On." Jesus challenges his disciples to be the "salt of the earth" and says he wants to set the world on fire with his message of salvation. We are invited to join in this work. Where do we begin? The smallest spark can ignite a great fire. This is a good week to ask yourself where God wants you to share your gifts. Where are the gifts of the Spirit in your life ready to be ignited so that you can spread the love of God to others in your family, workplace, neighborhood, and beyond? Where is the oven that needs you as the catalytic agent? Where can God use you to bring light and heat to a world that is otherwise dark and cold? Be ready and open to respond this week.

OTHER READINGS: JEREMIAH 38:4–6, 8–10; HEBREWS 12:1–4

TWENTY-FIRST SUNDAY IN ORDINARY TIME

ENTER THROUGH THE NARROW DOOR

LUKE 13:22–30

²² He passed through towns and villages, teaching as he went and making his way to Jerusalem. ²³ Someone asked him, "Lord, will only a few people be saved?" He answered them, ²⁴ "Strive to enter through the narrow door, for many, I tell you, will attempt to enter but will not be strong enough. ²⁵ After the master of the house has arisen and locked the door, then will you stand outside knocking and saying, 'Lord, open the door for us.' He will say to you in reply, 'I do not know where you are from.' ²⁶ And you will say, 'We ate and drank in your company and you taught in our streets.' ²⁷ Then he will say to you, 'I do not know where [you] are from. Depart from me, all you evildoers!' ²⁸ And there will be wailing and grinding of teeth when you see Abraham, Isaac, and Jacob and all the prophets in the kingdom of God and you yourselves cast out. ²⁹ And people will come from the east and the west and from the north and the south and will recline at table in the kingdom of God. ³⁰ For behold, some are last who will be first, and some are first who will be last."

Be Vigilant! Lectio Divina for Year C

Jesus continues on his journey toward Jerusalem. At this point in the Gospel Jesus's teachings are direct, forceful, and often challenging. In our reading, Jesus the teacher is challenged by a religious expert and his answer shocks his Jewish audience. The question is how many people will be saved. It was commonly asked of religious leaders in this period. The author of one Jewish apocryphal book of the time writes: "This age the Most High has made for many, but the age to come for a few" (4 Ezra/ 2 Esdras 8:1). And in the Jewish compendium of religious teaching known as the Mishnah (200 BC—200 AD) the rabbis are in general agreement that at the end of time only a "remnant" of Jews would be saved.

Rather than simply answer the stock question, Jesus issues an existential challenge: Those who wonder about salvation statistics should "strive to enter through the narrow door, for many … will attempt to enter but will not be strong enough." The Greek word translated as "strive" is *agonizomai,* the source of "agonize" in English. Jesus is saying that there is real work to be done, effort to be made. Faith requires action. No one is getting into the heavenly banquet based on their reputation or group membership.

Then Jesus places his listeners into an end-of-time scenario. When the master of the house (God) gets up and locks the door, his decision is final. He will hear soulful pleading from "you" to open the door. But the master will send them away, saying "I do not know where you are from." Some cultural background reveals why this response is so harsh. In the Middle East, knowledge of a person is based on two things—who your father is and where you come from. Do your family and village have honorable reputations? When the master sends the supplicants away by saying he doesn't know where they are from, he is saying that these "evildoers" are not living up to the honorable expectations he had set for them. They are no longer welcome in his home to share the intimacy of table fellowship.

In this scenario those who are rejected by the master stand outside in grief and anger as they peer in and witness the banquet of the faithful. They see Abraham, Isaac, Jacob, and all the other prophets of God feasting while they are left out. And still others have been invited to join the master in celebration. These interlopers are obviously Gentiles. They have been called from the four cardinal directions to attend the celebration and all of them have their own seat at the banquet. These "last ones" are now first. The first—the religious leaders of Jesus's time—had their opportunity to respond but now find themselves at the end of the line. The first have become last, and now they are locked out.

Meditatio

How many will find their way through the narrow door to the feast on the other side? We get glimpses in Revelation 7. John reports his vision of an assembly of men and women welcomed into God's embrace. He learns from his angelic guide that the number of Jewish believers marked with the "seal" of God as saved is 144,000 from Israel's twelve tribes. This representative number is intended by the author to be understood exponentially, as complete and beyond calculation. John then looks deeper into the vision and is witness to more who are saved—"a great multitude, which no one could count, from every nation, race, people, and tongue." A vast multitude of Gentiles have come to faith in Jesus as the promised Messiah of Israel. They have been drawn to the Lord from the north, the south, the east and the west. John sees these, together with the 144,000, standing before the throne and caught up in the eternal praise of God.

In 1 Timothy 2:4 St. Paul teaches that God "wills everyone to be saved and to come to knowledge of the truth." Does he mean that everyone will be saved? No. But it does mean that God will bring as many to salvation as possible. God's grace abounds, as pervasive as sunlight. We can put up an umbrella and block the source but the source—grace—still remains. This is our consolation this week. Everyone can be saved. That is God's will. Some may choose not to respond to God's grace, but many others will.

Will you be among their number? Our role is to be open to the moments of grace that call us to God and the heavenly banquet and so join the company of those Jewish and Gentile believers who have passed through the narrow door.

Oratio

Lord, give me strength and courage this week as I strive to enter through the narrow door that leads to life. I know that a banquet is waiting on the other side. I long to join Abraham, Isaac, Jacob, and a host of others who all gather to celebrate your victory over the grave.

——————————— *Contemplatio* ———————————

What can we do about our own salvation? What kind of response can be made this week? St. Paul calls us to work out our salvation with "fear and trembling" (Philippians 2:12–13). Salvation is a gift, but it is not a given. Jesus warns his hearers that they can find themselves on the outside looking in if they try to enter on the strength of their own merits or on their religious reputation. Faith demands action, but these actions need to be motivated by our faith. Christians are called to feed the hungry, clothe the naked, visit the sick, and encourage those in despair. These (among others) are known as the "corporal works of mercy." Engaging in any (or all!) of these faith-inspired actions helps keep us in contact with the God who created us to love and serve others with our unique spiritual gifts, natural talents, and personal treasure. Look for opportunities to serve this week, motivated by the teaching of St. Paul, as opportunities to "work out your salvation." You are not trying to secure it but to work out of it, in dedicated concern for others expressed through your acts of kindness.

OTHER READINGS: ISAIAH 66:18–21; HEBREWS 12:5–7, 11–13

TWENTY-SECOND SUNDAY IN ORDINARY TIME

WHO GETS THE PLACE OF HONOR?

LUKE 14:1, 7–14

[1] On a sabbath he went to dine at the home of one of the leading Pharisees, and the people there were observing him carefully.

[7] He told a parable to those who had been invited, noticing how they were choosing the places of honor at the table. [8] "When you are invited by someone to a wedding banquet, do not recline at table in the place of honor. A more distinguished guest than you may have been invited by him, [9] and the host who invited both of you may approach you and

say, 'Give your place to this man,' and then you would proceed with embarrassment to take the lowest place. [10] Rather, when you are invited, go and take the lowest place so that when the host comes to you he may say, 'My friend, move up to a higher position.' Then you will enjoy the esteem of your companions at the table. [11] For everyone who exalts himself will be humbled, but the one who humbles himself will be exalted." [12] Then he said to the host who invited him, "When you hold a lunch or a dinner, do not invite your friends or your brothers or your relatives or your wealthy neighbors, in case they may invite you back and you have repayment. [13] Rather, when you hold a banquet, invite the poor, the crippled, the lame, the blind; [14] blessed indeed will you be because of their inability to repay you. For you will be repaid at the resurrection of the righteous."

Lectio

Jesus accepts an invitation to dine in the home of an important Pharisee on the sabbath. The host seems to have invited a big group to join the meal and witness him hosting the well-known teacher. Jesus realizes that they are all watching him carefully. His reputation as an engaging guest and a disrupter of social customs is well known, and he does not disappoint here.

People in this culture recline around a low table to eat, and the arrangement of the guests reflects their relative social standing. Jesus notices the other guests maneuvering anxiously for positions of honor around the table. The two seats next to the host are particularly coveted. This jostling sparks the creative mind of the Lord. He fashions a parable to challenge the invited guests—and their host.

When you respond to an invitation and arrive at a great wedding feast, do not seek the places of highest honor, even if they are available. If you do, and someone of higher status appears, you will face public shame when the host asks you to take a lower place. It is worth noting that the "lowest" place at a table was only two places to the left of the host (this is where Judas reclined at the Last Supper). Taking the "highest" place, immediately to the left of the host, you run the risk of being shamed by moving only one place to your left. But if you take the lowest place to begin with, you might then be invited to move next to the host. In this way you can avoid any shame and may gain honor. It is worth the risk.

Now Jesus turns his attention to his respected host, the Pharisee. He gives him countercultural instructions for the next time he hosts a community meal. Instead of inviting his social, economic, and political peers, he should rather invite the poor, the crippled, the blind, and the lame. Your peers can repay you in kind, but the poor will never be able to do so. To invite these types of people would be social suicide. Yet Jesus promises the Pharisee that if he invites the socially disenfranchised to dine with him he will be repaid for this kindness by the Father in heaven.

Where would he find the poor, the crippled, the blind, and the lame to invite to a feast? They would have been lining the road outside his home that very night, ready to receive alms that might be gifted them by those invited to this feast. Before the guests depart any leftover food is distributed to these people, who in turn praise the goodness of the host, honoring him publicly for this generosity. The guests would leave the Pharisee's home listening to the praise of the host on the lips of the grateful poor. It is a win/win for host, his guests, and the poor alike.

This is the challenge of the parable. Jesus the guest is telling his host how to do his job better next time. Will any of the guests respond to Jesus's advice and move to a lower place around the table? Will the host consider inviting those who cannot repay in kind to his next sabbath meal? Our writer does not record the listeners' response. Our challenge is to put this teaching to the test the next time we attend or host a meal. God knows our hearts and will bless us for our effort to take the lowest place and to honor the poor, the crippled, the lame, and the blind in our lives.

─────────── *Meditatio* ───────────

"Give your place to this man." Those words would be difficult for anyone to hear, no matter the context, time, or culture. We work hard to find the best seats at restaurants and theaters. We pay extra for better airplane seats. My wife and I purchase movie tickets online to choose seats that best enhance our viewing pleasure. Some of us actually make the effort to arrive early to church so that we can secure our favorite seats in the sanctuary.

How would you feel if a person in authority told you to move and give your seat to someone else. Would you resist? Would you argue? Would you go willingly? Would your response be one of anger? Frustration? Shame? These are questions worthy of our meditation this week.

Oratio

Our prayer response comes from a passage in Proverbs 25:6–7 that the Pharisee and his guests had ignored: "Claim no honor in the king's presence, nor occupy the place of superiors; For it is better to be told, 'Come up closer!' than to be humbled before the prince." *Lord, it will take the gift of spiritual courage to take the lowest place. I pray that I can find the courage to respond to your teaching and leave the places of highest honor to others so that you can be exalted in my life.*

Contemplatio

These teachings of Jesus are not some spiritual calculation but a way of life. His teaching is as countercultural now as when he first spoke. Will we choose to accept or avoid its challenge? Open your heart to the spiritual practice of looking for the lowest place. Let God show you where you should sit, or whom you should invite. It will be very clear. You will know when the time comes what seat to take and whom you could honor with alms and an invitation. The promise of Jesus remains: "The one who humbles himself will be exalted" in the eyes of Jesus, in the eyes of the Father, and in the eyes of the church. Give it a try this week and see how it goes.

OTHER READINGS: SIRACH 3:17–18, 20, 28–29; HEBREWS 12:18–19, 22–24a

---

> ## TWENTY-THIRD SUNDAY IN ORDINARY TIME

COSTLY GRACE

LUKE 14:25-33

[25] Great crowds were traveling with him, and he turned and addressed them, [26] "If any one comes to me without hating his father and mother, wife and children, brothers and sisters, and even his own life, he cannot

be my disciple. [27] Whoever does not carry his own cross and come after me cannot be my disciple. [28] Which of you wishing to construct a tower does not first sit down and calculate the cost to see if there is enough for its completion? [29] Otherwise, after laying the foundation and finding himself unable to finish the work the onlookers should laugh at him [30] and say, 'This one began to build but did not have the resources to finish.' [31] Or what king marching into battle would not first sit down and decide whether with ten thousand troops he can successfully oppose another king advancing upon him with twenty thousand troops? [32] But if not, while he is still far away, he will send a delegation to ask for peace terms. [33] In the same way, everyone of you who does not renounce all his possessions cannot be my disciple."

Lectio

The crowds following Jesus grow larger each day, drawn to the excitement that surrounds his ministry of healing, preaching, and teaching. They experience the wonder of the miracles and the displays of his divine power. They delight whenever Jesus confounds and confuses the religious leaders who attempt to shame him with questions they hope will reduce him to silence. In our Gospel this week Jesus issues a strong challenge to those who want to join the movement and become his disciples. He will demand a level of commitment that most will find difficult to maintain.

Jesus is blunt: "If any one comes to me without hating his father and mother, wife and children, brothers and sisters, and even his own life, he cannot be my disciple" (verse 26). A disciple in this context is a student who is committed to a rabbi. Anyone who wants to follow Jesus must be willing to pay the price, and it may be higher than they first thought. The disciples of Jesus must be willing to carry the cross of their commitment.

By this point in his public ministry, association with Jesus would lead to persecution. This should not have surprised anyone who remembered the Sermon on the Mount. Jesus has promised that those who follow him would be "blessed," but in a way that they could not have imagined. His followers would be blessed when others "insult you and persecute you and utter every kind of evil against you [falsely] because of me." When so persecuted, you should "rejoice and be glad," for "thus they persecuted the prophets who were before you" (Matthew 5:11–12).

This is a high price. To follow Jesus would require a radical commitment of love. And in addition to carrying their own cross, potential disciples would also have to hate their fathers and mothers, sisters and brothers, and their own lives in order to follow Jesus. How is this possible? Why would Jesus make such a demand of potential disciples?

Does this sound like the teaching of the Messiah? It does if you understand how the words "love" and "hate" function in the Middle East. You love something, someone, your family when you are "attached" to them in relational support. Conversely, to hate someone simply means to detach yourself from dependence upon that relationship. Jesus is saying that to be his disciple your loyalty and dependence upon your family of origin has to end. This is the "cross" disciples must bear. You cannot serve two masters. The apostles are proving themselves worthy of this discipleship challenge. Later in Luke 18:24–30 they finally understand that what seems impossible with men is still possible with God. Peter and the other apostles have left homes, families, and their way of life to follow Jesus. They are detaching themselves from life in Galilee and have attached themselves to Jesus. The loyalty demanded by Jesus remained absolute.

Not everyone would make the grade. Jesus suggests that potential disciples take a moment to count the cost, do the math. Don't start building the tower or defending the castle unless you know your effort will end in success. Avoid the shame associated with failure. The stakes have never been higher, nor has the teaching about the cost of becoming a disciple been stated more clearly.

———————————— *Meditatio* ————————————

The relationship between teacher and student is different in the Middle East. A teacher takes on disciples to impart to them everything the teacher knows about a subject. This ensures that the master's command of the subject is passed to the next generation. The graduating students will recall, teach, and live what they have learned at the feet of the scholar. Even in the modern state of Israel, at Hebrew University in Jerusalem, doctoral degrees are conferred upon candidates in the Biblical Studies department only when a scholar-mentor determines that the student knows everything the teacher has ever learned. How long does that take? Until the teacher decides the process is complete. If your teacher dies before you finish, you start over with a new teacher. You are in for the long haul.

Jesus is doing the same thing with his disciples. They will be his witnesses after his resurrection and ascension to the Father. The future of the church depends on their radical commitment. We too are challenged to remove our attachments to our former way of living, our former sources of security and identity, and be born again into a new family of faith.

"If anyone wishes to come after me, he must deny himself and take up his cross daily and follow me. For whoever wishes to save his life will lose it, and whoever loses his life for my sake will save it" (Luke 9:23–24). Becoming and training to be a disciple is a high calling with a high reward—and a high cost: your livelihood, your loves, even your very life. Sit with these thoughts as you prepare to hear the Gospel this week.

––––––––– *Oratio* –––––––––

I found this prayer at followingjesus.org. It captures the desire of the heart to be a faithful disciple. *Lord, surround us with your love, fill us with your grace, and strengthen us for your service. Empower us to respond to the call of Jesus—to deny ourselves, to take up our crosses, and to follow. Make us your disciples. Amen*

––––––––– *Contemplatio* –––––––––

This week we face a real challenge. How do we respond to the call to renounce all we have so that we can be a disciple of Jesus? Someone once pointed out that you and I may be the only Bible some people ever read. Do we truly mirror the Lord in every aspect of our lives? Is the joy of the Lord our strength? What have you had to put aside in order to follow Jesus? Was it worth the cost? What have you depended on in the past that you left behind to follow Jesus? Wealth? Fame? Relationships? Leisure time? Your former reputation? Remember, there is no such thing as cheap grace. Everything comes at a cost. We are promised a cross when we sign on to follow the Lord. Authentic discipleship requires radical commitment. What will it cost you this week? What is the cross you bear? Pay the price, carry the weight, and anticipate the joy that will be yours when you hear from Jesus, "well done, good and faithful servant."

OTHER READINGS: WISDOM 9:13–18b; PHILEMON 9–10, 12–17

TWENTY-FOURTH SUNDAY IN ORDINARY TIME

PARABLES OF THE LOST

LUKE 15:1–10 (11–32)

¹ The tax collectors and sinners were all drawing near to listen to him, ² but the Pharisees and scribes began to complain, saying, "This man welcomes sinners and eats with them." ³ So to them he addressed this parable. ⁴ "What man among you having a hundred sheep and losing one of them would not leave the ninety-nine in the desert and go after the lost one until he finds it? ⁵ And when he does find it, he sets it on his shoulders with great joy ⁶ and, upon his arrival home, he calls together his friends and neighbors and says to them, 'Rejoice with me because I have found my lost sheep.' ⁷ I tell you, in just the same way there will be more joy in heaven over one sinner who repents than over ninety-nine righteous people who have no need of repentance.

⁸ "Or what woman having ten coins and losing one would not light a lamp and sweep the house, searching carefully until she finds it? ⁹ And when she does find it, she calls together her friends and neighbors and says to them, 'Rejoice with me because I have found the coin that I lost.' ¹⁰ In just the same way, I tell you, there will be rejoicing among the angels of God over one sinner who repents."

━━━━━━ *Lectio* ━━━━━━

The three parables in Luke 15 share a common theme: Something lost is found: a sheep, a coin, a son (or two; look back to the Fourth Sunday of Lent, "Two Sons" on page 65). When what was lost is returned to its rightful place the response is great joy. This week I will address the first of the three, the parable of the lost sheep.

Let's visualize the scene that inspired Jesus to teach these parables. Tax collectors and other "sinners" are gathering around a common table to eat with Jesus and listen to him teach. This is too much for the Pharisees and the teachers of the law who stand nearby. For them, *feeding* sinners is praiseworthy but *eating* with them is forbidden. Food was shared from common bowls and all dipped their bread in the same vessels. We can sense the agitation. These men—supposedly the shepherds of the community—are publicly reacting with shock and disdain.

Jesus tells these grumblers a parable that also engages the outcasts. He introduces the main character, a shepherd. At that time shepherding was a dishonorable and ritually unclean trade. Shepherds routinely left their women unprotected at night to be with their flocks. They were also considered thieves because they allowed their sheep to graze in fields that did not belong to them. Yes, Moses and David were both shepherds, but they were exceptions.

Jesus wonders if any of his listeners would leave a flock of ninety-nine valuable animals in the care of hired men to go out and search for a single lost sheep. The expected answer: "No! I would not! Seeking lost sheep is perilous—and besides, I didn't lose that sheep. That sheep lost me!" People in the Middle East have a distinctive take on personal responsibility. Once an employee in Jerusalem explained to me why he was late for work. He did not miss the bus. He had every intention of being on that bus, but "the bus missed him." He didn't assume any personal responsibility for his tardiness. The bus did not cooperate with his plans. From his perspective this explanation made perfect sense. Now we can understand how a shepherd in the time of Jesus might ignore the fact that a sheep had gone missing. The shepherd didn't lose that sheep. That sheep lost the shepherd. That cultural background brings out the shock element in the story.

Jesus's good shepherd does leave the ninety-nine and go in search for the lost animal. He knows the sheep has become "cast down." A friend of mine is a professional shepherd and explained the process to me. Due to the weight of its fleece, a fallen animal can end up with its feet in the air, unable to get up and return at the shepherd's call. It loses circulation in its legs. The sheep begins to bleat helplessly, hoping the shepherd will find it and restore its ability to walk. Its plaintive cry is easy to hear and follow by the shepherd—and by local predators.

In the parable the shepherd risks life and limb to save this animal. He sets out, listening for the bleating. When he finds the sheep, he has to act quickly because now both of them are in danger from predators. The animal weighs too much for him to carry it all the way back to the village, but he quickly hoists the sheep on his shoulders and begins to run in place, watching for wolves. This allows him to use his shoulders to help pump the blood that has drained into the sheep's thorax back down to its legs. After about ten minutes the task is completed and the cast-down sheep is restored and can follow him back to the flock.

When the shepherd arrives there is great rejoicing in the village. They know he took a great risk to find, restore, and return the lost sheep. With great risk comes great reward. Jesus promises there will be similar rejoicing in heaven when even one sinner repents.

—————————————— *Meditatio* ——————————————

In Psalm 23 David imagines God as a shepherd. The psalm is written from the perspective of a sheep who trusts completely in the shepherd. The good shepherd ensures that it will never lack for anything. It is led to green pastures to graze. It is provided with drink from quiet waters, not from the coursing streams that spring up after the occasional desert rains. The shepherd seeks lost animals who have become cast down and "restores their souls." The sheep knows that goodness and mercy will pursue it all the days of its life and that it will dwell in the house of its shepherd forever.

God is that good shepherd who will always seek and find the lost no matter the cost. His sheep know that he will lay down his life for any member of the flock. God is heroic, brave, relentless, and full of compassion. Give this some thought as you prepare to hear the Gospel proclaimed and preached this weekend. If you have time, also read the discussion of shepherds in Ezekiel 34. Do you think Jesus had this in mind when talking with the Pharisees?

In Psalm 23 David recalls his time as a young shepherd. Three verses will serve as our prayer response to the Gospel. Ask the Lord to make them true for you this week:

"The LORD is my shepherd; there is nothing I lack. In green pastures he makes me lie down; to still waters he leads me; he restores my soul. He guides me along right paths for the sake of his name." (Psalm 23:1–3)

Big risk. Big reward. The shepherd is willing to risk everything to seek, find, and restore a lost animal to his flock. His response is compassionate, courageous, and purposeful. Who is a lost sheep in your family? Among your group of friends? In your community? In your church? Listen. Is God calling you to take steps to find and restore this person? A call, an email, a text would mean a lot to anyone who is "cast down" in life and unable to find their way home. Remember the lesson of the parable. Big risk, big reward. Be open to anyone who may be lost this week. Be ready and willing to do what it takes to bring them home.

OTHER READINGS: EXODUS 32:7–11, 13–14; 1 TIMOTHY 1:12–17

TWENTY-FIFTH SUNDAY IN ORDINARY TIME

EVERYONE WINS!

LUKE 16:1–13

[1] Then he also said to his disciples, "A rich man had a steward who was reported to him for squandering his property. [2] He summoned him and said, 'What is this I hear about you? Prepare a full account of your stewardship, because you can no longer be my steward.' [3] The steward said to himself, 'What shall I do, now that my master is taking the position of steward away from me? I am not strong enough to dig and I am ashamed to beg. [4] I know what I shall do so that, when I am removed from the stewardship, they may welcome me into their homes.' [5] He

called in his master's debtors one by one. To the first he said, 'How much do you owe my master?' ⁶ He replied, 'One hundred measures of olive oil.' He said to him, 'Here is your promissory note. Sit down and quickly write one for fifty.' ⁷ Then to another he said, 'And you, how much do you owe?' He replied, 'One hundred kors of wheat.' He said to him, 'Here is your promissory note; write one for eighty.' ⁸ And the master commended that dishonest steward for acting prudently.

"For the children of this world are more prudent in dealing with their own generation than are the children of light. ⁹ I tell you, make friends for yourselves with dishonest wealth, so that when it fails, you will be welcomed into eternal dwellings. ¹⁰ The person who is trustworthy in very small matters is also trustworthy in great ones; and the person who is dishonest in very small matters is also dishonest in great ones. ¹¹ If, therefore, you are not trustworthy with dishonest wealth, who will trust you with true wealth? ¹² If you are not trustworthy with what belongs to another, who will give you what is yours? ¹³ No servant can serve two masters. He will either hate one and love the other, or be devoted to one and despise the other. You cannot serve God and mammon."

—— *Lectio* ——

The parable of the dishonest manager is unique and has baffled interpreters from the days of Jesus until now. Perhaps some cultural insights will assist us in our study, meditation, and contemplation this week.

Each character in the parable has something to gain. The rich man owns large tracts of land that he rents out to tenant farmers for a profit. They broker their contracts through his employee-agent, the steward or estate manager. This middleman has authority from the owner to set the rents the tenants will pay when the growing season ends. The steward is paid directly by his employer—and also by "under the table" gratuities given in exchange for more favorable rental agreements. The tenants assume that the absentee owner trusts his agent and believes that he is acting in his best interest. This is not the case in this parable.

The steward has been caught red handed and charged with mismanagement. He is summoned and accused, and does not speak a word in his own defense. He is guilty and knows it. There is no excuse or escape. He is informed of his termination and ordered to turn in a summary of the accounts the next day. Here we find the "shock" element of the parable. The steward is dismissed but is not in jail. He knows that his employer is stern and has judged his actions accurately. He is no longer in his employ. But the steward has learned something else about the rich man: He is merciful. He has not cast him into debtors' prison. He is free to act on his own behalf, at least for the time being. He will have to act quickly.

The tenant farmers are shocked to see the steward back in the village. The charges they levied against the man were serious. He should be in jail, but here he is standing before them as a free man. The steward has a plan. He intends to meet with each renter individually. On the pretext that he has some good news to share, he invites them to come into his office one at a time. Each person is asked what he owes the master. Each renter is directed to reduce his bill by an average of 500 denarii, or 500 days' wages.

The tenants pay rent on large tracts of land, indicated by the amount of wheat and oil they owe the rich man. Now their debt has been significantly reduced. What's going on? Is *this* the way the owner is expressing his regret for finding out so late in the game that his estate manager has been cheating them? There is an immediate celebration in the village. The good news about this unexpected windfall spreads far and wide. Everyone sings the praises of the generous landowner. The honor of the rich man increases exponentially. Everyone wins!

Now the other shoe drops. The steward returns to the master the next day. The master realizes that he has "cooked the books." His "merciful" response to his estate manager resulted in this unintended consequence. He has lost a lot of money but has also gained the praise of his tenants. His honor status has never been higher. His steward has tricked him but in a manner so clever that the master has to praise him before he kicks him out of his office. Praise him? For his obvious deceit? No. He is praised for acting prudently. The steward devised and implemented a plan that benefited all three characters in the parable. The renters rejoice over their unexpected financial windfall. The steward himself is owed a debt of gratitude from the tenants who believe he went to bat for them. He told them he secured the rent reduction from the owner on their behalf. They will have a chance to repay him later when he is looking for another job. The master is celebrated in the village for his generosity in reducing the amounts owed to him that year. Everyone wins!

<hr>

Meditatio

Jesus's ability to use unsavory characters in some of his parables grabs our attention and keeps us engaged. He teaches about prayer by introducing us to an unjust judge who does not fear God or man yet renders a favorable verdict for a poor widow who is persistent in her plea for justice. A friend at midnight is ordered to go away by an uncooperative neighbor who won't get up and unlock the door to provide bread for a guest until the friend's persistence (and the real possibility of public shaming in the morning) compels him to rise and give him what he needs. And then there is the younger son who sees his father as dead in his eyes, shaming his father by demanding his inheritance. That same son is welcomed back and celebrated by his father. He was dead but came back to life.

The unsavory character here comes through the test unscathed. A Christian in the West might ask why Jesus would choose a dishonest person to be the hero. The Eastern Christian might wonder why anyone would criticize him. The steward should be praised for acting so quickly and with such confidence to preserve his life after being removed for his misdeeds. He learned something about his employer when he was fired. His master is just, but he is also merciful. The steward, to his credit, does not offer lame excuses for his behavior. This leads to him being released and ordered to bring the accounts back the next day. The steward leaned into the master's kindness and acted to preserve himself before the news of his being fired reached the village. If the master in the parable is a God-figure (and I think he is) then our meditation should begin with a reflection on how the mercy of God might temper judgment. It might be better to say nothing and then act to bring honor to God with our actions. The rich man in the parable is impressed with this clever fellow. He took care of himself, blessed the renters with a rate reduction, and increased the honor status of the master. Not bad for a day's work.

In Psalm 86 the psalmist reminds us that God is both kind and merciful. Verse 15 is our prayer response this week. *"But you, Lord, are a compassionate and gracious God, slow to anger, abounding in mercy and truth."* Amen.

Win, win, and win. All three characters in the parable come out as winners this week. How often in life does that actually happen? The biggest winner is the "dishonest steward." He "acted prudently." That means that he acted quickly to ensure that his plan would benefit others beside himself. He based his trust on the God-figure in the parable. His employer was as rich in mercy as he was stern in his judgment. The steward gambled everything on this mercy. He was not in jail. He had freedom to act. How could he provide for his master, for himself, and everyone else in the village as well?

That should be our goal this week. Look for opportunities and implement plans that will result in a win/win for you and others.

OTHER READINGS: AMOS 8:4–7; 1 TIMOTHY 2:1–8

TWENTY-SIXTH SUNDAY IN ORDINARY TIME

AT HIS DOOR

LUKE 16:19-31

[19] "There was a rich man who dressed in purple garments and fine linen and dined sumptuously each day. [20] And lying at his door was a poor man named Lazarus, covered with sores, [21] who would gladly have eaten his fill of the scraps that fell from the rich man's table. Dogs even used to come and lick his sores. [22] When the poor man died, he was carried away by angels to the bosom of Abraham. The rich man also died and was buried, [23] and from the netherworld, where he was in torment, he raised his eyes and saw Abraham far off and Lazarus at his side. [24] And he cried out, 'Father Abraham, have pity on me. Send Lazarus to dip the tip of his finger in water and cool my tongue, for I

am suffering torment in these flames.' [25] Abraham replied, 'My child, remember that you received what was good during your lifetime while Lazarus likewise received what was bad; but now he is comforted here, whereas you are tormented. [26] Moreover, between us and you a great chasm is established to prevent anyone from crossing who might wish to go from our side to yours or from your side to ours.' [27] He said, 'Then I beg you, father, send him to my father's house, [28] for I have five brothers, so that he may warn them, lest they too come to this place of torment.' [29] But Abraham replied, 'They have Moses and the prophets. Let them listen to them.' [30] He said, 'Oh no, father Abraham, but if someone from the dead goes to them, they will repent.' [31] Then Abraham said, 'If they will not listen to Moses and the prophets, neither will they be persuaded if someone should rise from the dead.'"

— *Lectio* —

We meet two characters in this parable. The "rich man" (read "greedy" rather than "rich") is extremely wealthy. Purple garments were outrageously expensive because the color was so difficult to extract. Purple dye was painstakingly sourced from the murex, a tiny sea snail. Extracted one drop and one shell at a time, even a small amount of dye required harvesting millions of shellfish. Garments dyed purple were so costly they were owned only by the elites in the Roman world. Our rich man also wears a fine linen garment underneath his purple outerwear—delicate, soft, and likewise costly. Additionally, we learn that he dines "sumptuously" each day. These meals constituted feasts and would have been attended by many well-heeled guests. This preoccupation with appearance and his luxury lifestyle does not bode well for him as the parable continues.

The second character in the parable has a name: Lazarus. This name speaks volumes. Lazarus is a Greek form of the Hebrew Eliezer which roughly translates to "the one God helps." We first meet Lazarus lying at the gate of the rich man's compound. He is placed there each day by members of his family. His obvious infirmity qualifies Lazarus as an almsworthy candidate. Guests arriving at the daily feasts would have been motivated to contribute alms toward his wellbeing as required in the law of God. The religious duty of a Jewish person was threefold: to pray daily, to fast one day annually, and to give alms to all almsworthy persons. Giving alms was a "mitzvah," and generosity would result in a blessing returned to you at a later time. God was always watching.

In the parable, Lazarus is in dire straits. His physical needs are obvious to everyone yet only the household dogs help alleviate his suffering. Lazarus longs to eat the scraps that fall from the rich man's table. These "scraps" were the pieces of bread used as napkins. Shared bowls of sauces made for messy fingers. Bread used to clean the fingers was discarded on the floor where the house dogs found the morsels. It was also the social responsibility of the wealthy to prepare more food than guests could consume. At the end of the feast the excess fare would be distributed to the deserving poor who waited outside and who would return praise to honor the generosity of the host. All of this is lost on our rich man.

Now the plot thickens. Both Lazarus and the rich man die. Lazarus is carried by angels to the comfort of Abraham's bosom while the rich man is buried. The rich man finds himself tormented by the fires of hell, separated from Abraham and Lazarus by a great chasm. The rich man recognizes Abraham and now seems to know Lazarus by name. He had ignored his religious duty toward Lazarus in life but now seeks pity from Abraham and suggests that he order Lazarus to provide a drink of water to cool his tongue. That will not be allowed. Father Abraham informs him that his fate is final and that no one can cross the chasm between them.

The once-rich man still does not understand. If Lazarus will not be allowed to serve him as a slave to slake his thirst, then perhaps he could be sent as a messenger to warn his five brothers about their impending doom if they do not repent. Abraham reminds him that they have Moses and the prophets. The rich man perisists and tries to enjoin Father Abraham to send Lazarus back from the grave. *That* will be the convincing proof they need! But Abraham is clear: If they will not listen to Moses and the prophets, they will not be persuaded even if someone should rise from the dead. The parable ends, leaving our minds in doubt about its precise meaning and affording us the perfect opportunity for our meditation this week.

Abraham responds to the rich man by reminding him that his five brothers have "Moses and the prophets. Let them listen to them." How would Moses and the prophets speak to his wayward siblings? What are the brothers of the rich man supposed to hear that he somehow missed?

"Moses and the prophets" refers to the Torah (the first five books of the Hebrew Bible) and the rest of the writings of Old Testament Scripture. The Torah offers clear and concise teaching about a believer's daily concern and necessary care for the poor, the widow, and the orphan. Passages like Exodus 22:21–22 and Deuteronomy 10:17–19 among countless others remind the Jewish person of faith of the religious and social responsibility owed to the least in the community. The prophets speak in clear tones about God's judgment that will come upon the nation because of the neglect of the needs of the disenfranchised poor. This is conveyed clearly in Jeremiah 5:27–29 and in many other passages.

The challenge is to listen and to act. The rich man knew his obligation to share his bounty with the poor who were placed at his gate. God had blessed him so that he could bless others. He did not respond to this obvious need. He faces the shame without any remorse. The rich man had his reward, but the blessings of Lazarus are going to be eternal. The chasm that separates the rich man and Lazarus is real, and it still exists. We only have an opportunity on this side of the divide to bless and serve by our generosity and love those who depend on God.

— *Oratio* —

Lord, open my eyes so that I can see you in the face of the poor. Show me a Lazarus this week whom I can comfort with a gesture of service and care. Amen.

— *Contemplatio* —

Are you a rich man or are you a Lazarus? There have been times in my life that I acted more like the rich man than I care to admit. I recall times of plenty when I neglected the needy who were at my door. There have been times when I could identify more as Lazarus. He was in pain, in need, dependent on the kindness of others to help him make it through the day. We are meant to find ourselves in these stories. They remind us that we all face an eternal destiny that is chosen on this side of the grave. Our faith in action will always draw us closer to God and to one another.

Our faith challenge this week is to be aware of a Lazarus in your life. Pray. Be bold and ask the Lord to reveal how you can reach out and provide the comfort and care for that person in your local community. It could be through efforts of direct service or by a charitable contribution to a particular outreach. We bear the Christian responsibility to act on what we believe. Serve a Lazarus this week for Jesus.

OTHER READINGS: AMOS 6:1a, 4–7; 1 TIMOTHY 6:11–16

TWENTY-SEVENTH SUNDAY IN ORDINARY TIME

INCREASE OUR FAITH!

LUKE 17:5–10

5 And the apostles said to the Lord, "Increase our faith." 6 The Lord replied, "If you have faith the size of a mustard seed, you would say to [this] mulberry tree, 'Be uprooted and planted in the sea,' and it would obey you.

7 "Who among you would say to your servant who has just come in from plowing or tending sheep in the field, 'Come here immediately and take your place at table'? 8 Would he not rather say to him, 'Prepare something for me to eat. Put on your apron and wait on me while I eat and drink. You may eat and drink when I am finished'? 9 Is he grateful to that servant because he did what was commanded? 10 So should it be with you. When you have done all you have been commanded, say, 'We are unprofitable servants; we have done what we were obliged to do.'"

Lectio

The opening words of our Gospel jump off the page! The apostles appeal urgently to Jesus: "Increase our faith." What did Jesus say to prompt this energized response?

Jesus has just informed his disciples that if they are going to follow his teachings and put them into practice they will need to forgive each other, perhaps multiple times and repeatedly. He is adamant: Even if your brother or sister sins against you seven times in a single day you must forgive the offense if he or she repents and expresses sorrow. This is a difficult teaching, especially among a group of disciples with no biological family ties. Immediate family members would have been expected to forgive each other's sins. But Jesus's disciples are expected to do even more.

Thus their cry for help: "Increase our faith." Why do they need more faith? We might imagine them asking instead for an increase of patience or endurance. But the Greek *pistis* that translates as "faith" has a deeper meaning than simple belief. It conveys a sense of loyalty and reliability that would be expected of familial relationships. Jesus is building a new family of followers. He expects them to relate to one another as members of the same family. The apostles realize they will need more faith to be as loyal and reliable to these new brothers and sisters as they have been to their own blood siblings.

Jesus responds with a powerful image of a mustard seed. The apostles need only a little more faith—the size of a tiny mustard seed—to achieve their goal. With this they will demonstrate to the rest of the community the kind of ongoing forgiveness that Jesus expects from all who follow him.

Jesus promises that with this tiny increase of faith they will be able to (figuratively) command a mulberry tree to be uprooted and planted in the sea. This image provides an excellent case study for making the important distinction between literal and literary interpretation. The image is meant to be understood in a non-literal manner. The apostles will not be granted the authority to uproot a tree and replant it in the sea! However, they will have the faith necessary to do the seemingly impossibly work of forgiving non-family members among the disciples as many times as needed.

———————————— *Meditatio* ————————————

"Increase our faith!" How is that even possible? It may help to understand that biblical faith is a threefold proposition. It begins with knowledge. To that knowledge you add belief, and to belief you add the final element of trust. When all three are operating together you have arrived at biblical faith. It seems that trust is the most elusive of these three. Trust is the "mustard seed" that Jesus refers to in the Gospel. This small yet vitally important element of the equation is what transforms the life of a believer.

Imagine yourself in a boat on the Sea of Galilee as a storm rages. Jesus approaches you, walking on the surface of the churning waves. Like the apostle Peter in Matthew 14:22–32, you recognize the Lord and hear him invite you to step out of the boat and walk above the waves to him. You respond. You clamber over the side of the rocking vessel. Standing on the water, you make your way toward Jesus. He waits for you joyfully. It took great faith for you to step out of the boat. The storm is violent, yet you are confident Jesus will provide all of your needs.

Suddenly your faith falters. You recognize the impossibility of what you are doing. You sink, slowly, crying out to Jesus, "Lord, save me!" He does. Standing with Jesus on the sea he says to you, "Oh you of little faith, why did you doubt?" Are you hurt? Embarrassed? Confused? You stepped out of the boat. You walked on the waves! You made your way to Jesus and now stand in his embrace. How can this be evidence of a lack of faith? It's not. Jesus used those words to encourage Peter. He had come so close to complete success. He lacked the last bit of faith, the element of trust that would have put him over the top. Jesus is commending Peter, not castigating him for lack of effort. The apostles in the Gospel are asking Jesus for that last bit of faith, for the complete trust they knew they will need to forgive anyone more than once. Let this be our meditation and prayer this week. "Lord, increase our faith."

Oratio

In Mark 9:20–24, Jesus comforts a distraught father whose son is intent on harming himself. He believes that Jesus can restore his son but still wavers in his faith. Jesus wants to heal his son. His response to Jesus will be our prayer response this week.

Lord, grant me the mustard-seed increase in faith that I will need to trust in you and your good plan for my life this week. "I do believe; help my unbelief!"

What if your faith increased the size of a mustard seed? Biblical faith carries the expectation of loyalty and reliability in our relationships such as those found among members of the same family. This faith-based loyalty is rare among those not related by blood. But we, you and I, *are* related. We are members of a new family—the Body of Christ. God is our father and Jesus our older brother. We are related by our common confession and are expected to be loyal and reliable in our relationships. Especially when it comes to forgiveness. If the first apostles were concerned about how they were going to forgive their new brothers and sisters, knowing they would need an increase of faith to get the job done, then we will too.

Forgiveness, loyalty, reliability. Each of these values is an important marker of a strong, well-knit, functioning family. Are these the hallmarks of our faith family? Are these three values of communal well-being experienced in the way that we relate to each other as members of the family of God? Make an effort to work on these three "family of faith" values: forgiveness, loyalty, and reliability within your church community this week.

OTHER READINGS: HABAKKUK 1:2–3; 2:2–4; 2 TIMOTHY 1:6–8, 13–14

TWENTY-EIGHTH SUNDAY IN ORDINARY TIME

THEY WERE CLEANSED

LUKE 17:11-19

[11] As he continued his journey to Jerusalem, he traveled through Samaria and Galilee. [12] As he was entering a village, ten lepers met [him]. They stood at a distance from him [13] and raised their voice, saying, "Jesus, Master! Have pity on us!" [14] And when he saw them, he said, "Go show yourselves to the priests." As they were going they were cleansed. [15] And one of them, realizing he had been healed, returned, glorifying God in a loud voice; [16] and he fell at the feet of Jesus and thanked him. He was a Samaritan. [17] Jesus said in reply, "Ten were cleansed, were they not?

Where are the other nine? [18] Has none but this foreigner returned to give thanks to God?" [19] Then he said to him, "Stand up and go; your faith has saved you."

Lectio

As our Gospel passage opens Jesus is approaching Judea, having passed along the eastern border of Samaria on his way from Galilee to Jerusalem. He is greeted by calls for mercy from a group of ten biblical lepers. I use the term "biblical" purposefully. The disease we know as classical leprosy or Hansen's disease did not exist in the time of Jesus. These ten people are afflicted with some sort of unattractive and likely contagious skin discoloration, and are legally forbidden from contact with others. But they are obviously devout, and believe that Jesus can restore them with a word.

Jesus hears them crying out from a respectful distance. They cannot come near for fear of contaminating Jesus and his disciples. Jesus tells them to "show yourselves to the priests," and they do; each leaves the scene to find the specific priest who had originally diagnosed his condition and pronounced his exclusion. The law required anyone healed from leprosy (however unlikely it might be) to return to the same priest, who would examine them again and pronounce their restoration. This healing would be as much a witness to the attending priest as to the lepers themselves.

One of the ten lepers unexpectedly returns. He is healed. He knows Jesus is God's agent. He throws himself at his feet and thanks him profusely. Jesus wonders where the other nine went. Why didn't they return to give thanks like this foreigner? This may make more sense than it appears. In the Middle Eastern world, you often refrain from saying thank you because the phrase can be considered dismissive. Especially in commerce, it suggests that you no longer have need of the person. If you say thank you to a merchant, it can imply, "Your service was not sufficient and I will no longer shop here!" A more helpful phrase is, "I will see you tomorrow, yes?" That conveys a loyal customer's satisfaction.

This former leper, a Samaritan, is about to leave the border lands to find the Samaritan priest who originally diagnosed his condition. Since Samaritans and Jews do not associate with each other, he knows he will never see Jesus again. He wants to thank Jesus before he returns home. The other nine are Jews. They are also overjoyed and on their way home so their priests can begin the process of their restoration to their families. Perhaps they don't come back and express gratitude now because they will see Jesus again. Jesus is heading to Judea and Jerusalem, and they are too.

Meditatio

Jewish priests had something of a community health function. Exclusion from the community was serious, so no one could be banished without careful examination, diagnosis, and quarantine. After a final determination, outcasts could not return home until the same examining priest was convinced they were healed. In Leviticus 14 we learn the seven-day process those who are healed must undergo to be given a clean bill of health. The ritual concludes with a compelling liturgical gesture. The attending priest takes some of the blood from the sacrificial doves and anoints the lobe of the right ear, the thumb of the right hand, and the big toe of the right foot of the person who had been healed. What is the meaning behind this sign? The right ear lobe, right thumb, and right big toe are signed with blood (and then with anointing oil) as a form of prayer. The action captures the idea that this person will now return to hearing, doing, and walking in the ways of the Lord. The person is whole again.

I love religious rituals. They convey so much more meaning and emotional reassurance than a simple pronouncement of healing by a religious or medical authority figure. Rituals take time, and sometimes they can be expensive (baptisms, weddings, funerals), but they are worth the effort. The community understands the message: We are reconnected with God.

Oratio

In the spirit of thanksgiving we turn to the Lord in prayer. We recall the words of the psalmist in Psalm 136:1–3. I imagine each of the ten healed lepers rejoicing while singing this psalm of praise.

> "Praise the LORD, for he is good; for his mercy endures forever;
> Praise the God of gods; for his mercy endures forever;
> Praise the Lord of lords; for his mercy endures forever."

We know that politics can create strange bedfellows, but this Gospel story shows that suffering does too. These ten lepers were drawn together by shared infirmity. They were outcast Jews and Samaritans, compelled by their exile to ignore their normal cultural and religious divides to form a new community of suffering. When they are healed by Jesus they will each return home to their native villages. They will never see each other again.

My mother died from an aggressive form of cancer at age sixty-three, a real and unexpected loss. In the course of treatment she sought any and all options that might bring healing. She told me that she was delighted to find herself part of a new community of people with her form of cancer. It was odd to be thrown into a mix of people from different backgrounds, races, and faith traditions with cancer their common bond, but she found this association of "lepers" compelling. Her treatment required a monthly trip to gather with others in a trial program some distance away. She never knew who would be there in a given month. Absences marked friends who had been cured or had died. In either case she knew she would never see them again. She told me she missed them, missed that close-knit community, even if the bond was their shared cancer.

Our faith response this week? Pray for those in similar situations. Maybe you know them, maybe not. Pray and ask the Lord to heal and restore. Visit if you can. Call when you get a chance. But by all means pray.

OTHER READINGS: 2 KINGS 5:14–17; 2 TIMOTHY 2:8–13

TWENTY-NINTH SUNDAY IN ORDINARY TIME

WILL HE BE SLOW?

LUKE 18:1-8

1 Then he told them a parable about the necessity for them to pray always without becoming weary. He said, 2 "There was a judge in a certain town who neither feared God nor respected any human being.

³ And a widow in that town used to come to him and say, 'Render a just decision for me against my adversary.' ⁴ For a long time the judge was unwilling, but eventually he thought, 'While it is true that I neither fear God nor respect any human being, ⁵ because this widow keeps bothering me I shall deliver a just decision for her lest she finally come and strike me.'" ⁶ The Lord said, "Pay attention to what the dishonest judge says. ⁷ Will not God then secure the rights of his chosen ones who call out to him day and night? Will he be slow to answer them? ⁸ I tell you, he will see to it that justice is done for them speedily. But when the Son of Man comes, will he find faith on earth?"

Lectio

Jesus loves to teach in parables. He uses these memorable stories to teach larger groups of people, especially those he may never address again. In this week's Gospel Jesus teaches about the importance of persistence in prayer. Two characters appear in a public setting, a city gate or public square. A local judge is hearing cases. He claims neither to fear God nor respect any person. He is a consciously shameless figure, unusual but still familiar in the honor-based culture of the New Testament. He would be called a "robber judge" because everyone knows that in his court "justice" follows the highest bidder. This judge believes himself immune from the social expectations of his role and even from the curse promised in Deuteronomy 27:19 on "anyone who deprives the resident alien, the orphan, or the widow of justice!"

The second character is a helpless widow. In Hebrew the word for "widow" is literally "the silent one," for widows in the ancient Middle East had no voice in public forums. With no husband to speak on her behalf and protect her from harm she is being taken advantage of and wants to press a case against her adversary. In the time of Jesus, she would have no way to address this issue in a public court, in front of a judge. But she can in the parable; that is a shocking element for the listening audience to consider. It is a reminder that God himself chooses to defend widows. In Psalm 68:6 the psalmist reveals God as Father of the fatherless and the defender of the widow.

Our widow has the daring that can come from desperation. She summons the courage to enter a public court and demand justice. The fact that she addresses a single judge suggests her case is financial, that her adversary is trying to wrest from her what little means she still controls. In the time of Jesus solitary judges would sit in judgment over financial dealings. Rebuffed, she returns again the next day and the next.

The robber judge is willing to ignore the widow for a time, but eventually she wears him down. We can assume that her cause is just. The judge's self-reflective response to her persistence is revealing. He admits to himself that she is straining his patience. Her constant cry for justice has caused him to reconsider his own self-interest. The widow is victorious! Too poor even to bribe the judge, she still prevails over her adversary. We learn that the judge is finally motivated by fear that the widow will come to "strike" him. The term is strong; despite his protest that he is not worried about what God or others think about him, the judge decides to avoid the social "black eye" she will cause him if her persistence is not rewarded. The widow is in the right and everyone in the community knows it.

The parable affords Jesus the opportunity to make a comparison between the delay of the robber judge and the timing of God. Jesus teaches his disciples that his Father will secure the rights of "his chosen ones" who are persistent in their prayer, day and night. They will get the justice they are due. That is good news. Finally, Jesus wonders if he will find such faithful persistence when the time of justice comes. Will the returning Son of Man find the kind of faith demonstrated by the widow in her persistent, constant, and eventually fruitful effort to secure a just decision against her adversary? It is still an open question today.

—————————— *Meditatio* ——————————

For our meditation this week, consider the contrast Jesus makes between the robber judge and the righteous God. The fictional judge is shameless because he doesn't care about anyone other than himself. The widow is nobody to him—but he ultimately caves to public pressure and does the right thing. Does God need the pressure of shame to act consistently with his character and help those he has chosen? The question answers itself.

Who is the parallel with the widow? The "chosen ones" of God. That's us! We are someone to God. God knows us and knows the justice we desperately need. And God is not bothered by us when we "call out to him day and night." When no one else will listen, he will both listen and answer.

Oratio

"Out of the depths I call to you, LORD; Lord, hear my cry! May your ears be attentive to my cry for mercy" (Psalm 130:1–2).

Contemplatio

Persistence in prayer. What does that mean for you and me? Are we to be as bold, as brash, and as persistent in our prayer life before the Lord as this widow before the judge? I think so, especially when our cause is just, our intent honorable. In the parable the defenseless widow demands justice against a merciless adversary. The Bible teaches that God is clearly on her side. Every day. All day long. Her witness of persistence is meant for us. We are challenged by Jesus to stand up for what is just and right. He promises that the Father will respond to these prayers.

Spend time this week practicing persistence in prayer. Start with the prayer that Jesus taught his disciples. The "Our Father," prayed persistently, will help you realize just how much the Father has already provided and wants to provide for your future. Your cause is just; this prayer is pure. "Forgive us our sins as we forgive those who have sinned against us." Be persistent in prayer and you will see the fruit of the Spirit grow in your life.

OTHER READINGS: EXODUS 17:8–13; 2 TIMOTHY 3:14—4:2

THIRTIETH SUNDAY IN ORDINARY TIME

'O GOD, BE MERCIFUL TO ME, A SINNER'

LUKE 18:9–14

⁹ He then addressed this parable to those who were convinced of their own righteousness and despised everyone else. ¹⁰ "Two people went up to the temple area to pray; one was a Pharisee and the other was a

tax collector. [11] The Pharisee took up his position and spoke this prayer to himself, 'O God, I thank you that I am not like the rest of humanity—greedy, dishonest, adulterous—or even like this tax collector. [12] I fast twice a week, and I pay tithes on my whole income.' [13] But the tax collector stood off at a distance and would not even raise his eyes to heaven but beat his breast and prayed, 'O God, be merciful to me a sinner.' [14] I tell you, the latter went home justified, not the former; for everyone who exalts himself will be humbled, and the one who humbles himself will be exalted."

Lectio

Luke the Evangelist frames the parable in our Gospel story this week so that his Gentile readers will have enough context about Jewish ritual and prayer to apply the parable to their own lives. Two men make their way up to the temple area to pray. They are not alone. Hundreds, perhaps thousands, would be making the same journey, anticipating the atonement offerings made at 9 a.m. and then again at 3 p.m. each day. This is not a time for private devotions. The daily ritual in Herod's temple is a liturgical drama complete with vested priests, sacrificial offerings, the offering of incense, and a public prayer before a final blessing and dismissal.

They are praying aloud at the time appointed during the liturgy, just as the incense is offered on the altar and the smoke rises into the heavens. The liturgy is designed so worshipers unite their prayer with this cloud of incense. Each man prays aloud and can easily be heard by the other. The question, though, is whether their prayer is heard by God.

The genius of Jesus is hidden in the description of their body language. First, we hear the prayer of the Pharisee, who has taken up a particular pose apart from everyone else. He classifies other people, and especially the tax collector, among the *am-haaretz*—the "people of the land," who are sinners and therefore unclean. Strict observers of the law would avoid physical contact with this sort of person to avoid becoming defiled. His stated intent is to remain in a state of ritual purity so that he can be available to be used in God's service.

Jesus points out that the pious Pharisee is actually praying to himself rather than to God, giving thanks that he is not like everyone else. They are "greedy, dishonest, and adulterous"—or even worse, like the tax collector. The Pharisee fasts twice a week when the Torah only required you to fast one single day each year, on Yom Kippur. The Pharisee pays tithes on all he has when the Torah requires tithes only on grain, wine, and olive oil. He is proud that he goes above and beyond the requirements in an effort to impress God. But where is the evidence of his service to his fellow man? He seems to despise them all, especially the tax collector.

The tax collector—a collaborator with the Roman occupation—probably earned his reputation. But tax collectors were capable of faith too. John the Baptist received and baptized tax collectors who wanted to know how they could continue in their profession and still please God. The Baptist challenged them and their hired soldiers to assess only what was authorized and to avoid extortion and false accusation. They were to be content with their pay (Luke 3:12–14). The tax collector is also standing apart from the others in the temple, but he is voicing a heartfelt prayer. He stands, eyes cast down, and uses his fists to beat his breast repeatedly as he prays: "O God, be merciful to me, a sinner." He goes home justified, not the seemingly pious Pharisee. The Pharisee's prayer never made it off the temple mount. The prayer of the tax collector was joined with the prayers of the assembly and rose to heaven. He returns to his home a new man.

───────────────────── *Meditatio* ─────────────────────

We can learn a great deal about prayer in Jesus's day as we pay attention to details in his parables. Public prayer could be heard by God and also by those nearby. The tax collector beats his breast as he repeats his prayer: "O God, be merciful to me, a sinner." Beating of the breast is a gesture typical to women in the Middle East. In anguished prayer they will often make a fist and beat their breast three times. Men also beat their breasts when praying, but only in times of extreme anguish. In Luke 23:48, for instance, the men and women who witness the brutal spectacle of crucifixion return to their homes "beating their breasts," overcome with grief. It is a powerful moment to imagine.

This week try to picture the proud Pharisee. He stands apart from the others with eyes and hands raised toward heaven, reminding God how much better he is than everyone else. Now find the tax collector in your mind's eye. Watch as he too stands alone, but with eyes cast down, beating his breast in anguished longing to experience the mercy of God. He is a sinner and desperately wants to be forgiven. He returns home justified. And the Pharisee? He is not justified. He exalted himself and so is humbled by God. The reversal is complete. The proudly pious lose their place to the humble, who are lifted up to the Lord.

Oratio

The apostle Paul teaches that believers should "pray without ceasing" (1 Thessalonians 5:17). The Eastern Church took this directive to heart and created the "Jesus Prayer," adapted from the prayer of the tax collector. This prayer is simple and repeatable. It is one way we can "pray without ceasing." Give it a try: "Lord Jesus Christ, Son of the living God, have mercy on me, a sinner."

Take a breath as you speak the words "Lord Jesus Christ, Son of the living God" and exhale on the words "have mercy on me, a sinner."

Contemplatio

How do you pray? Where do you pray well? When do you pray well? What postures or spiritual practices appeal to you in your prayer life? We can ask ourselves these questions this week as we seek a faith response to the Gospel. I am a Catholic Christian. When it comes to public prayer, we have all the bases covered. We stand and pray. We sit and pray. We strike our breasts three times in prayer. We kneel and pray. We raise our hands and pray. Our prayer is communal and personal. There are times (during the prayers of intercession) that we hear other people's prayers and also times when we pray aloud together. All of my senses are engaged in prayer. I see the prayer on the page. I read the prayer aloud. I change my posture in prayer during the service. I stand, sit, and kneel in prayer.

Be especially aware of how you pray well and where you pray well to enter into the experience of prayer more fully this week.

OTHER READINGS: SIRACH 35:12–14, 16–18; 2 TIMOTHY 4:6–8, 16–18

I MUST STAY AT YOUR HOUSE

LUKE 19:1-10

[1] He came to Jericho and intended to pass through the town. [2] Now a man there named Zacchaeus, who was a chief tax collector and also a wealthy man, [3] was seeking to see who Jesus was; but he could not see him because of the crowd, for he was short in stature. [4] So he ran ahead and climbed a sycamore tree in order to see Jesus, who was about to pass that way. [5] When he reached the place, Jesus looked up and said to him, "Zacchaeus, come down quickly, for today I must stay at your house." [6] And he came down quickly and received him with joy. [7] When they all saw this, they began to grumble, saying, "He has gone to stay at the house of a sinner." [8] But Zacchaeus stood there and said to the Lord, "Behold, half of my possessions, Lord, I shall give to the poor, and if I have extorted anything from anyone I shall repay it four times over." [9] And Jesus said to him, "Today salvation has come to this house because this man too is a descendant of Abraham. [10] For the Son of Man has come to seek and to save what was lost."

Lectio

On his way to Jerusalem, Jesus travels through Jericho. He does not plan to stop here. As he enters the city he restores the sight to a blind man soliciting alms at the city gate. This display of healing power attracts a huge crowd that surrounds Jesus as he does his best to make his way across the city. In the Middle East you do not lead a procession from the front. His disciples surrounded Jesus, forming a sort of human shield, ready to close ranks at any threat. Progress through Jericho's narrow streets would be safe—but slow. Everyone in town would know that a VIP is passing through and would want to see the great prophet from Galilee, Zacchaeus among them. Unfortunately, he is "short in stature" and cannot see over the crowds. His vast wealth is no help here.

He has wealth because Zacchaeus is a "tax agent," not a mere "tax collector." He hired tax collectors like Matthew to do the work of extracting funds from the local population to replace the heavy tax assessment he paid to Rome. He profited by extorting additional funds from his fellow Jews and is hated for being a willing servant of Rome. One scholar describes his tax business as a combination of a Ponzi scheme and protection racket. He is essentially a public enemy and if found unprotected might certainly fear for his life.

Zacchaeus's decision to run ahead and go outside of the city is foolhardy. His hasty plan is to secretly climb one of the sycamore fig trees planted just outside the city gate complex. These large trees produce a canopy of big leaves, and their deep shade is appreciated by those who wait in the sun each day for the gates to be opened. He thinks his plan is working perfectly. Jesus comes by the tree and Zacchaeus can see him clearly, but then Jesus stops! Jesus notices him and immediately calls for Zacchaeus—by name—to come down, and says that he must stay at his house that night. He has changed his plans and will stop in the city after all. The city fathers are in shock. The crowds grumble. Why would Jesus eat in the home of such a well-known sinner? It doesn't make sense. Or does it?

To prepare and serve such a large meal on sudden notice would challenge any household. Even though Zacchaeus is a wealthy man with hordes of servants, it will take time to secure and prepare the animals needed to feed such a large group of unexpected guests. During the time of preparation and throughout the course of the meal Jesus has ample opportunity to converse with his host and challenge him with his message of salvation. At the end of the meal we discover that Zacchaeus is a new man. He begins publicly to make amends for stealing from his fellow Jews and appeasing the Roman overlords.

Zacchaeus's conversion is authentic. Half of his possessions given to the poor is the most allowed by Jewish law. The other half of one's estate had to be left for his immediate family. He begins to divest himself of his ill-gotten funds. It even seems that he intends to collect no more taxes. He is done with his life of sin. Jesus welcomes him as a disciple, delighted to name him as a son of Abraham who was lost and has now been found.

Meditatio

What does it mean to be a son of Abraham? The patriarch in the book of Genesis has an engaging storyline. His life of faith features both success and failure. He begins his journey as a pagan who leaves his idols behind and responds to the call of God to leave his family and go to a new land. He falls into sin along the way, and several times God has to intervene to right the wrongs of a patriarch who threatened to put the plan of salvation at risk. But in the end Abraham comes through. He obeys God even when doing so seems to be absurd; he is directed to sacrifice his only son Isaac, the son of the promise God made to him. His faith is credited to him by God, and so he is called the father of faith.

As disciples of Jesus we are also sons and daughters of Abraham. We also have been invited to become members of the family of God. Read through Genesis 12–22 this week. These chapters help reveal what Jesus means when he calls Zacchaeus a son of Abraham. See if you can find yourself in these chapters as well.

Oratio

Look to Psalm 116:12–14 as we draw on these verses for our prayer response this week. "How can I repay the LORD for all the great good done for me? I will raise the cup of salvation and call on the name of the LORD. I will pay my vows to the LORD in the presence of all his people." Amen.

Contemplatio

There is a special blessing when we gather around a common table to share a meal. It is around a table with Jesus that Zacchaeus repents of his ways, starts to divest himself of his ill-gotten wealth, and becomes a disciple.

This would be a good week to plan a meal to share with people you know and love. We are all trained to avoid discussing religion or politics at table. But what about faith? Take time around the table to have each person share their story of faith. You go first. Share how you came to know the Lord and how that encounter changed your life. Who knows? It may be that there will be a Zacchaeus around your table, too. Bon appétit!

OTHER READINGS: WISDOM 11:22—12:2; 2 THESSALONIANS 1:11—2:2

EVEN MOSES

LUKE 20:27–38

²⁷ Some Sadducees, those who deny that there is a resurrection, came forward and put this question to him, ²⁸ saying, "Teacher, Moses wrote for us, 'If someone's brother dies leaving a wife but no child, his brother must take the wife and raise up descendants for his brother.' ²⁹ Now there were seven brothers; the first married a woman but died childless. ³⁰ Then the second ³¹ and the third married her, and likewise all the seven died childless. ³² Finally the woman also died. ³³ Now at the resurrection whose wife will that woman be? For all seven had been married to her." ³⁴ Jesus said to them, "The children of this age marry and are given in marriage; ³⁵ but those who are deemed worthy to attain to the coming age and to the resurrection of the dead neither marry nor are given in marriage. ³⁶ They can no longer die, for they are like angels; and they are the children of God because they are the ones who will rise. ³⁷ That the dead will rise even Moses made known in the passage about the bush, when he called 'Lord' the God of Abraham, the God of Isaac, and the God of Jacob; ³⁸ and he is not God of the dead, but of the living, for to him all are alive."

— *Lectio* —

A group of Sadducees approaches Jesus and challenges him with a question related to their particular understanding of Jewish law. These religious leaders hold a minority position and deny the possibility of a bodily resurrection after death. They recognize only the Torah as inspired, and those first five biblical books, they claim, offer no clear teaching about resurrection. In Acts 23:8, Luke reminds his readers that "the Sadducees say that there is no resurrection or angels or spirits, while the Pharisees acknowledge all three." Jesus's teachings are more aligned with the Pharisees.

The Sadducees ask Jesus to imagine a scenario based on Deuteronomy 25:5–10, the law of levirate marriage. There, Moses teaches that when brothers live together and the married brother dies without producing a male heir, his younger (unmarried) brother is bound to marry the widow and produce a son to carry the name of the deceased so that it will "not be blotted out from Israel." If the brother refuses to honor this obligation, the widow can press charges. If convicted, the widow would be allowed to shame him publicly, to "strip his sandal from his foot and spit in his face"!

The Sadducees draw on this little-used law to ridicule the idea of resurrection. What if there were a woman who marries seven brothers in succession, all of whom die before she does. Whose wife will she be in the resurrection? Which of her seven husbands will she claim? The first? The last? The Sadducees may not believe in a bodily resurrection, but they do believe marriage is an eternal bond. Things would become quite confusing.

Jesus's response reveals his theological genius. He tells them that there is an important difference between people currently alive and those of "the coming age." Because of the commandment in Genesis 1:28 to "multiply" and "fill the earth," a primary goal of marriage in Judaism is to bear children to replace those who will eventually die. But the age to come will no longer need replacement offspring. All who benefit from the resurrection of the dead can never die again. The grave will be conquered. Jesus says that in this way they will be like the angels—and of course Sadducees don't believe in angels either!

Jesus has a final insight that will silence them completely. Since the Sadducees are all about Moses, Jesus quotes Moses, and not from an obscure law but from Exodus 3, the key story of God's revelation of his name at the burning bush. God tells Moses that he is the God of Abraham, the God of Isaac, and the God of Jacob. Jesus asserts that God cannot be the God of the dead but only of the living, "for to him all of them are alive." It stands to reason that these three patriarchs are alive with God beyond the grave. How did they miss that fact? Silence is the only possible response from the Sadducees. Their attempt to shame Jesus has backfired spectacularly. Even nearby scribes (Pharisees to be sure) recognize Jesus's victory over his theological foes. They exclaim boldly, "Teacher, you have answered well" (verses 39–40).

Christians believe in bodily resurrection after death because of Jesus. He has conquered death and the grave and we will follow him. His resurrection after three days was corporeal and real. The earliest evangelists are careful to report that hundreds witnessed his resurrection and many others ate and drank with the Lord after he returned from the dead. The teaching about a bodily resurrection could not be compromised.

In 1 Corinthians 15:14, St. Paul reminds us that "if Christ has not been raised, then empty [too] is our preaching; empty, too, your faith." The doctrine of the bodily resurrection is central to what we believe. The earliest Christian martyrs went to their graves confident that they will be called back to life. The fear of death was also conquered when Jesus conquered the grave. Death no longer holds us captive. That is why we can pray with St. Paul when he says to death, "Where, O death, is your victory? Where, O death, is your sting?" Lean into these words of comfort this week.

Oratio

Our prayer response this week is an early Christian hymn found in Ephesians 5:14. Most likely recited at baptisms, it is a prayer that reminds us that life does not end in the grave; rather it begins! *"Awake, O sleeper, and arise from the dead, and Christ will give you light."*

Contemplatio

If I limit my study of Scripture to certain books or familiar passages, what do I miss? Do I need to pay more attention to the Hebrew Bible? The Old Testament contains insights that help me understand the teachings of Jesus in the New Testament. The Sadducees limited their biblical knowledge to the first five books of the Bible. The full collection of books in the Hebrew Bible could have provided them with so much more. I also need to expand my study and prayer beyond the Gospels and look for additional insight from the Lord in the rest of the New Testament. What am I missing in Hebrews, Jude, 1 and 2 Peter, 1 and 2 John, and the Revelation?

This might be a good time to begin a systematic reading program that will take you through the whole Bible, day by day, over the course of a year. You can find many different schedules of daily readings online. Ask the Lord to open your spiritual eyes, ears, and heart to the new insights and connections you will make along the way.

OTHER READINGS: 2 MACCABEES 7:1-2, 9-14; 2 THESSALONIANS 2:16—3:5

A TEMPLE OF THE HOLY SPIRIT

LUKE 21:5-19

[5] While some people were speaking about how the temple was adorned with costly stones and votive offerings, he said, [6] "All that you see here— the days will come when there will not be left a stone upon another stone that will not be thrown down."

[7] Then they asked him, "Teacher, when will this happen? And what sign will there be when all these things are about to happen?" [8] He answered, "See that you not be deceived, for many will come in my name, saying, 'I am he,' and 'The time has come.' Do not follow them! [9] When you hear of wars and insurrections, do not be terrified; for such things must happen first, but it will not immediately be the end." [10] Then he said to them, "Nation will rise against nation, and kingdom against kingdom. [11] There will be powerful earthquakes, famines, and plagues from place to place; and awesome sights and mighty signs will come from the sky.

[12] "Before all this happens, however, they will seize and persecute you, they will hand you over to the synagogues and to prisons, and they will have you led before kings and governors because of my name. [13] It will lead to your giving testimony. [14] Remember, you are not to prepare your defense beforehand, [15] for I myself shall give you a wisdom in speaking that all your adversaries will be powerless to resist or refute. [16] You will even be handed over by parents, brothers, relatives, and friends, and they will put some of you to death. [17] You will be hated by all because of my name, [18] but not a hair on your head will be destroyed. [19] By your perseverance you will secure your lives."

The church year is drawing to a close. This week we hear from the "end times" account in Luke's Gospel. As the disciples rest after the ascent to the temple mount, they call attention to the temple's impressive stones and the beautiful gold decorations and carvings on its walls. The response of Jesus leaves them in shock. He predicts a time when every one of these stones will be thrown down! "Teacher," they ask, "when will this happen? And what sign will there be when all these things are about to happen?"

Jesus replies in the present tense. He declares that the temple will be destroyed within their lifetime! In Luke 21:32 Jesus makes this clear when he says, "Amen, I say to you, this generation will not pass away until all these things have taken place." A biblical generation lasts forty years. Jesus makes this prediction in AD 32 and the temple is reduced to rubble by the Romans before the year 72. Forty years. What are the signs the disciples need to watch for?

Jesus uses "apocalyptic" or "end-times" language in this pronouncement. This language must be read spiritually, not literally. Every warning of Jesus is fulfilled completely in advance of the temple's destruction. So what will happen before the temple is destroyed? What does Jesus have to say about all of this?

He warns that in the next forty years others will come "in my name," claiming "I am he." False messiahs were common in this period. For example, we have Barabbas, who is named in all four Gospels. Barabbas is not a name but a title that translates "bar" to "son" and "abba" to "father." Barabbas claimed to be "the Son of the Father," the Messiah.

Jesus warns the disciples that they will hear of wars and rumors of war, but they should not be afraid. And indeed, we read in our histories of the internal decay of the Roman empire and provincial rebellions, including that of the Jews, who declared war on Rome in AD 66.

And what of the predicted earthquakes, famine, and pestilence? In the year AD 44 a severe famine struck a large portion of the Roman Empire. This famine was predicted by the Christian prophet Agabus in Antioch (see Acts 11:27–30). And in AD 60 the cities of Colossae, Laodicea, and

Hierapolis were leveled by earthquakes. Ancient Colossae still lies in ruins. In AD 62 the Roman city of Pompeii was destroyed by an earthquake.

And then comes the final warning that religious and civil authorities will persecute the disciples. They would lay hands on the disciples and deliver them to synagogues where they would be tried, convicted, and cast into prison. Jesus promises that some would stand before kings and governors to witness to Jesus. All of these predictions were fulfilled not least in the ministry of St. Paul.

The temple was finally destroyed by Roman armies under general Titus. A traditional story says that the general was displeased no Christians were in the city when the temple fell. They had heeded Jesus's warning and fled in advance of the Roman arrival, waiting out the storm in safety across the Jordan River in Pella.

Meditatio

Jesus is not making predictions in this passage about the end of the world but about the destruction of the Jerusalem temple, the house of God where sacrifices were offered daily for the forgiveness of sin, where Jews came to celebrate the feasts of Passover, Pentecost, and Tabernacles. The temple, and all it stands for, is ending. This will clear the way for a new temple, as the Spirit of God comes to reside in the heart of each believer.

St. Paul reminds the Corinthians that each one of them has a body that "is a temple of the Holy Spirit within you" (1 Corinthians 6:19). This is the same Spirit that Jesus promised to send his disciples, when he taught that the Spirit of truth will be in them (John 14:15–17). Every believer is now a temple of the Holy Spirit. God lives in you and me. Inspired and empowered by the Spirit, we can now spend our lives doing the great works of God. We continue the witness of our ancestors in faith as we share the light of Christ in a world darkened by sin. Let your light shine this week!

Oratio

This week we join in the prayer of the apostle John in Revelation. Each day we are one day closer to our own end time.

"The one who gives this testimony says, 'Yes, I am coming soon.' Amen! Come, Lord Jesus!" (Revelation 22:20).

As a student at Fuller Seminary I saw a bumper sticker on a professor's car that read, "Jesus is coming soon! Look busy!" I chuckled then and still do. One day Jesus will return to judge the living and the dead. Try not to get entangled in attempts to figure out the day, time, or hour. Jesus reminds us that this is reserved to God alone and not for you and me to know.

I take comfort in 2 Peter 3:8–9: "With the Lord one day is like a thousand years and a thousand years like one day. The Lord does not delay his promise, as some regard 'delay,' but he is patient with you, not wishing that any should perish but that all should come to repentance." God's math suggests that in reality we have only been waiting for a couple of days for the Lord's promised return as judge. And we may have to wait a couple more. Rejoice in the fact that each passing day and hour is another opportunity for grace to influence men and women to respond to an invitation to relationship with Jesus, a relationship that can transform their lives forever. So remember: "Jesus is coming soon! Look busy!" Do the work of an evangelist, sharing your faith with someone new this week.

OTHER READINGS: MALACHI 3:19–20a; 2 THESSALONIANS 3:7-12

OUR LORD JESUS CHRIST, KING OF THE UNIVERSE

REMEMBER ME WHEN YOU COME INTO YOUR KINGDOM

LUKE 23:35-43

[35] The people stood by and watched; the rulers, meanwhile, sneered at him and said, "He saved others, let him save himself if he is the chosen one, the Messiah of God." [36] Even the soldiers jeered at him. As they approached to offer him wine [37] they called out, "If you are King of the Jews, save yourself." [38] Above him there was an inscription that read, "This is the King of the Jews."

³⁹ Now one of the criminals hanging there reviled Jesus, saying, "Are you not the Messiah? Save yourself and us." ⁴⁰ The other, however, rebuking him, said in reply, "Have you no fear of God, for you are subject to the same condemnation? ⁴¹ And indeed, we have been condemned justly, for the sentence we received corresponds to our crimes, but this man has done nothing criminal." ⁴² Then he said, "Jesus, remember me when you come into your kingdom." ⁴³ He replied to him, "Amen, I say to you, today you will be with me in Paradise."

Lectio

Our Gospel reading begins as Jesus arrives at the site of his execution. The executioners are swift and efficient. In a matter of minutes he is nailed to a cross, crucified between two others. It is a horrific way to die. Breaking the victim's spirit was just as important to the Romans as breaking his body. The crucified person could survive for several days. It was common during this time of prolonged agony for victims to curse God and others, begging for death.

People stand and watch. Why do they subject themselves to this graphic display of state-sponsored torture? In truth it could not be avoided. Roman crucifixion was a purposefully public event. Criminals were left hanging just six feet above the ground along the roads leading into major cities. Jesus is crucified just outside one of the western gates of Jerusalem. Among the watchers are the religious leaders—the "rulers" in our Gospel account—who violently opposed all Jesus did and taught. They revile him while others watch quietly or pass by as quickly as possible.

Their public accusations show their desire to heap shame and scorn on him. "He saved others, let him save himself if he is the chosen one, the Messiah of God." Had Jesus saved others from death? Indeed he had. With the words *"talitha koum"* Jesus had called the daughter of a synagogue ruler back from the grave. More recently in Bethany Jesus had called his good friend Lazarus out of the tomb. The rulers wonder if Jesus will take advantage of this same divine power now.

Jesus has no response for them. His silence speaks volumes. The prophet Isaiah, writing about a suffering servant Messiah, says that although he was "harshly treated, he submitted and did not open his mouth; like a lamb led to slaughter or a sheep silent before shearers, he did not open his mouth" (Isaiah 53:7). The silence of Jesus in the face of these accusations is yet another proof that he is the Messiah, the Christ, the promised king.

The two men who are crucified with Jesus may have been disciples of Barabbas, the rebellion leader and false messiah. He and his followers had been arrested in an uprising and were scheduled for execution together. But Jesus had taken Barabbas's place on the cross (see Luke 23:18–25). One of the two criminals begins to revile Jesus. He follows the example of the religious leaders and challenges Jesus to take advantage of his divine ability to deliver them from death. He hears a stinging rebuke from his partner in crime: "Have you no fear of God?" Have you no shame? Their sentences are just, but he knows Jesus is innocent of any crime against Rome. He asks Jesus to remember him when the ordeal is over and Jesus comes into his kingdom. Jesus does. He promises him that today, that very day, he will be with him in Paradise.

Meditatio

Jesus hung on the cross under a sign that read, "This is the King of the Jews" (verse 38). The Romans meant it as mockery, but this week the church celebrates the Feast of Christ the King. What kind of king are we talking about? Would Jesus rule like a Herod? Like Nero? Never. Jesus explained what his kingdom is like when he taught his disciples that "The kings of the Gentiles lord it over them … but among you it shall not be so. Rather, let the greatest among you be as the youngest, and the leader as the servant.… I am among you as the one who serves" (Luke 22:25–27).

In the kingdom of God, the king washes the feet of the subjects and expects us to follow his example. This should be the way we look like Jesus, the way we celebrate the Feast of Christ the King as we wait in joyful hope for the second coming of our Lord and Savior Jesus Christ.

Oratio

This week, make the prayer of the "good thief" (as he is often called) your own. "Jesus, remember me when you come into your kingdom."

The good thief asks Jesus to "remember" him. What does he want Jesus to remember about him? The biblical idea of remembering is about more than remembering where I left my car or remembering to call my mother on her birthday. When we remember someone in the culture of the Bible, we do so to act on their behalf and to their benefit. When I want you to remember, it means that I want you to do something for me too! The good thief on the cross wants Jesus to remember him and come to his assistance. Jesus promises that he will, and that he will be welcome that same day in Paradise.

This is a good week to "remember" someone in this biblical way. Ask the Lord to show you who you need to remember. To complete the challenge, act on behalf of that person and deliver some blessing into their lives. Write them a letter, give them a call, or send them an email or a text. If appropriate, let them know that when you remembered them you felt God's Spirit move you to connect with them. Be open to these opportunities as you remember others this week.

OTHER READINGS: 2 SAMUEL 5:1–3; COLOSSIANS 1:12–20

MORE RESOURCES

ABOUT THE AUTHOR

Kevin Saunders is a Catholic Bible teacher in Phoenix, Arizona. He became particularly interested in the cultural world of Jesus while living in the Old City of Jerusalem. His popular Bible class can be found online at ArizonaBibleClass.com.

CATHOLIC MINISTRIES

For more on the practice of Lectio Divina, we recommend the book *Pray with the Bible, Meditate with the Word* (ABS Item 122590V), available on Bibles.com in English and Spanish.

American Bible Society's Catholic Initiatives offers resources in digital, video, and print formats. Visit us at catholic.americanbible.org.